D1557143

# COLONIAL MARYLAND NATURALIZATIONS

By
## Jeffrey A. Wyand
*&*
## Florence L. Wyand

*Baltimore*
GENEALOGICAL PUBLISHING CO., INC.
*1986*

Copyright © 1975 by
Genealogical Publishing Co., Inc.
Baltimore, Maryland
All Rights Reserved
1st Printing 1975
2nd Printing 1986
Library of Congress Catalogue Card Number 75-10681
International Standard Book Number 0-8063-0680-7
*Made in the United States of America*

For

C.S.W.

# FOREWORD

This collection of records developed from a search amongst naturalizations for genealogical information concerning some of the Germans who settled in western Maryland. In examining the records of eighteenth century naturalizations, valuable data beyond mere names and dates were discovered. The sole key to these records, a card index, was found to be incomplete and to contain serious errors. In order to add to the literature about the Germans who migrated to Colonial Maryland, this complete set of naturalizations granted according to two eighteenth century English statutes was extracted from Maryland's Provincial Court documents. Parliament intended the two naturalization laws to encourage Germans specifically, so long as they were Protestant, to emigrate to Maryland. But numerous non-German Protestant immigrants took advantage of the liberality of the laws to gain civil rights. Therefore, the compilation of those naturalization records, Part III of this volume, should assist genealogists and demographers whose interests lie both within and outside the German element.

An account of the English statute naturalizations provides an incomplete picture of the naturalization process in Colonial Maryland. Therefore, the extant recorded naturalizations accomplished by means other than the English laws have been included here. Part I of this book lists those immigrants who acquired limited rights of citizenship through denization during the seventeenth century. Part II provides the available information on persons who received naturalization via enactment of private bills by the colonial legislature.

The data of Parts I and II have previously been published, scattered throughout various volumes of the Maryland Archives. Part III consists of material which, with the exception of the names of 128 of the immigrants, has not heretofore appeared in print.

All of the entries in this volume have been carefully transcribed from the sources and checked for accuracy. Still it is difficult to eliminate error completely and the authors apologize for problems which may arise from their mistakes. Controversy may be resolved by consulting the referenced source, either the Maryland Archives volumes or the Court documents at the Hall of Records in Annapolis.

It is a pleasure to acknowledge the courteous and patient cooperation given to this project by the staff of the Hall of Records, particularly that of Mrs. Phebe Jacobsen and Mrs. Pamela Narbeth.

Annapolis                                          Florence Leone Wyand
April 1975                                              Jeffrey A. Wyand

## TABLE OF CONTENTS

INTRODUCTION

The Lords Baltimore recognized from the earliest settlement of their Province of Maryland that success depended, in nearly every respect, upon expansion of the population.  To encourage settlement, private citizens who paid the cost of transporting able-bodied males were offered rewards of land under the terms of the Conditions of Plantation.[1]  At first, there were no express limitations on whom might claim the rewards; but by 1642 the Conditions restricted claimants to those "of Brittish or Irish descent.[2]"  The change reflected the fear of placing lands and potential power in foreigners whose loyalty to Lord and King might not be undivided.  By 1649, however, Lord Baltimore was willing to relent slightly and he authorized his colonial representatives, in their discretion, to make grants of land to persons of French, Dutch or Italian descent who otherwise fulfilled the Conditions of Plantation then in force.[3]

The first application of the intent of the 1649 declaration arose not from the contemplated direct importation of aliens, but from one of the Baltimores' many boundary disputes.  The Swedish and Dutch settlers of the village of New Amstel on Delaware Bay were thought to be encroaching upon Proprietary lands.  Forcible expulsion of the putative intruders was suggested by some, but skillful negotiators,including Augustine Herman, the Bohemian cartographer of Maryland, prevailed.[4]  For their part of the agreement, some of

---

1 Aubrey C. Land, "The Colonial Period," in The Old Line State, A History of Maryland, Morris L. Radoff, ed. (Annapolis, 1971), p. 13.
2 Archives of Maryland, William H. Browne, et. al. eds. (Baltimore, 1882 - present), III, pp. 47, 99.
3 Ibid., III, p. 233.
4 Ibid., III, p. 428.  Deiter Cunz, The Maryland Germans, (Princeton, 1948), pp. 14ff.

the settlers, including Herman, moved to territory indisputably within Baltimore's jurisdiction. In return, Lord Baltimore conferred some property rights upon individual settlers, even though they were not born within the British dominions. The first of those conferrals of denization, an adaptation of a Royal power, was issued in 1660.[5] The recipients of the denizations acquired status well beneath that of the natural-born or naturalized citizen.

> A denizen is an alien born, but who has obtained
> ex donatione regis, letters patent to make him
> an English subject, a high and incommunicable
> branch of the royal prerogative. He may take
> lands by purchase or devise, which an alien may
> not; but cannot take by inheritance; for his
> parent, through whom he must claim, being an
> alien, had no inheritable blood; and therefore
> could convey none to the son. And upon a like
> defect of hereditary blood, the issue of a den-
> izen, cannot inherit to him; but his issue born
> after may. No denizen can be of the Privy
> Council, or either House of Parliament, or have
> any office of trust, civil or military, or be
> capable of any grant of land, etc., from the
> Crown.[6]

Lord Baltimore's denizations were only as broad as his sovereignty; his denizens' rights as to land, its acquisition and disposal, pertained only to Maryland. The letters of denization typically noted this limitation:

> ...And likewise any land Tenements Revenues
> Services and other heriditam'ts whatsoever with-
> in our said province of Maryland may inherite or
> or otherwise purchase receiue take haue hold buy

---

5 Denizations issued by the Provincial Council in the name of Lord Baltimore form Part I of the following work.
6 William Blackstone, Commentaries, I, p. 394, cited in Bernard C. Steiner, Citizenship and Suffrage in Maryland, (Baltimore, 1895), p. 7.

and possess and them may occupie and enjoy Giue
Sell alyen and bequeath as likewise all liber-
tyes franchises priuiledges of this our province[7]
...

The denizens soon became dissatisfied with their few property rights and sought greater opportunities. In 1666, James
Neale, an Englishman whose children had been born outside the
British dominions, desired to confirm his children's rights
of inheritance before undertaking another task in service of
the Crown. Neale pursued his goal by requesting passage of a
private naturalization measure by the Assembly and the Provincial Council. Augustine Herman followed Neale's lead and
filed a petition for himself, members of his family, and oth-
ers asking that they "...henceforth be adjudged reputed &
taken as Nrãll borne people of the Province of Maryland[8]..."
Herman pointed to the spirit of Lord Baltimore's declaration
of 1649 and warned that the failure to grant fuller rights of
citizenship than those of denization would result in "...
foreslowing the peopleing of this Province with usefull Arti-
ficers & handicrafts men[9]..." The legislature agreed and a
bill in Herman's favor was enacted the same day that Neale's
act was passed.[10] Thereafter legislative naturalization became firmly established and denization was doomed to wither.[11]
In addition to the denizen's rights, a legislatively-natural-

---

7 Archives of Maryland, III, p. 465.
8 Ibid., II, p. 144.
9 Ibid.
10 These and subsequent naturalizations accomplished by enactment of private statutes in Maryland form Part II of the
   work that follows.
11 The "traditional" denization process lasted only nine years
   more. A few vestigial denizations were granted by governors
   through the 1770's to confirm inheritable land titles in
   alien Catholics. Those denizations, which bypassed the
   eighteenth century religious oaths required for naturalization, were not recorded in official records and are not included here. An example of one of these vestigial denizations (for Peter Baker of Baltimore County) survives in the
   manuscript collection of the Maryland Historical Society.

ized citizen could, in Maryland,

> ...maintaine Prosecute Avow Justifie and defend
> All manner of Actions Suits Pleas Plaints and
> other Demands whatsoever, as Liberally, Frankly
> Freely, fully, Lawfully and Securely as if they
> ...had been Naturall born People and Subjects of
> this province[12]...

Although legislative naturalizations continued to be enacted for specific individuals, general naturalization statutes were rejected in 1669 and 1671.[13] A 1692 naturalization
statute merely set out the procedure that had been followed
up to that time: upon advice and consent of the Assembly and
the Council, the governor could administer an oath of alle-
giance to a settled alien and issue him letters patent making
him for "...all Intents and Purposes, fully and compleatly
Naturalized.[14]"

In 1735, a general naturalization statute of three year's
duration was enacted in Maryland, permitting the colonial
govenor to issue naturalizations without the approval of the
Assembly.[15] The general naturalization statute added the
oath of abjuration to the naturalization requirements. That
oath required each applicant for citizenship to pledge alle-
giance to the Protestant King and his successors and to repud-
diate the Pope, the doctrine of Transubstantiation, and the
claims of the Catholic James III, "the Old Pretender.[16]"
This statute was renewed twice, expiring in 1740.[17]

---

12 Archives of Maryland, XXXVIII, p. 133.
13 Steiner, Citizenship and Suffrage in Maryland, p. 10.
    Archives of Maryland, II, p. 249.
14 Archives of Maryland, XIII, p. 440. Thomas Bacon, Laws
    of Maryland at Large, etc. (Annapolis, 1765), Acts of
    1692, c.VI.
15 Archives of Maryland, XXXIX, pp. 287ff. Bacon, Laws of
    Maryland at Large, Acts of 1735, c.VII.
16 Bacon, Laws of Maryland at Large, Acts of 1716, c.V.
17 Archives of Maryland, XL, pp. 235, 343. No official re-
    cords of naturalizations under this statute or its exten-
    sions were located.

In 1740, Parliament finally took notice of the flow of non-English immigrants into the American colonies and adopted a measure under which those immigrants could acquire almost the same status as British subjects. Section I of the act, 13 Geo. II c.7, provided that those aliens who resided in America for seven consecutive years, without an absence that exceeded two months in duration, and who swore the anti-Catholic oath of abjuration (Quakers could affirm) before a colonial provincial court between 9 a.m. and noon, could be granted essentially all the rights of citizenship for a fee of two shillings.[18] Section II required each applicant, except Quakers and Jews, to present a certificate at court, attested by two witnesses, that he had been administered a Protestant communion within the preceding three months. Section III allowed Jews to omit the words "upon the true faith of a christian" in swearing the required oaths. Section IV authorized the issuance of a certificate of naturalization by the court. Section V ordered each colonial secretary to forward annually a list of those naturalized in his province to the commissioners of trade in London.[19] Parliament was soon made aware that the swearing of oaths was abhorrent to more of the American immigrants than the Quakers. In 1747, the statute 20 Geo. II c.44 relieved the "...Moravian brethren and other foreign protestants, not Quakers, who conscientiously scruple the taking of an oath..." of the oath tests.[20] Certificates of communion were still required and the political limitations

---

18 Danby Pickering, The Statutes at Large from the Ninth to the 15th Year of King George II (London, 1765), 17, pp. 370-373.
19 Those lists were the source material for M. A. Giuseppi, Naturalizations of Foreign Protestants in The American and West Indian Colonies, (Pursuant to Statute 13 George II c.7)(London, 1921). Either only one-eighth of the names of persons so naturalized in Maryland were ever transmitted to London or only that fraction of the total was extant in 1921.
20 Danby Pickering, The Statutes at Large from the 20th to the 23rd Year of King George II (London, 1765), 19, p. 143.

imposed by the 13 Geo. II c.7 statute were reiterated: those so naturalized were not eligible to sit in Parliament or any other higher council of the British government.  That political limitation presented no foreseeable difficulty for the Maryland immigrants, particularly for the Germans who were settling Maryland's backwoods.  The easing of the oath requirement meant that virtually all of the non-Catholic alien immigrants, even the Anabaptists, could, for the first time, acquire citizenship that was universal in the American colonies.[21]

This Parliamentary means of naturalization became the most popular method of acquiring rights of citizenship in colonial Maryland.  Maryland's Provincial Court granted citizenship to more than one thousand immigrants from 1742 to 1775 by this procedure.  The more limited legislative naturalization route remained available, but its use dwindled.

Few of the new citizens who followed the Parliamentary course of naturalization suffered from its political restrictions.  For example, Elie Vallete's Parliamentary naturalization of 1764 was a qualification, not a bar, to his service as the clerk of the Prerogative Court of Maryland from 1764 to 1777.[22]  But Jonathan Hagar, the founder of Hagerstown, Maryland, discovered that a different standard applied to elected office.  Following the precedent of the statute 12 & 13 William III c.2, the 13 Geo. II c.7 statute, under which Hagar was naturalized in 1747, disqualified Hagar and those

---

21 The universality of the procedure meant that the full seven year residency need not be completed in one colony and that the oaths need not be administered in the colony of residence.  Thus some Marylanders were naturalized in adjacent colonies and vice versa.  All the naturalizations issued in Maryland are recorded in Part III of the work that follows.  Pennsylvania naturalizations of Marylanders are found either in M. A. Guiseppi, op. cit., and/or in Pennsylvania Archives, 2nd series, vol. II.
22 Gust Skordas and Elizabeth Hartsook, Land Office and Prerogative Court Records of Colonial Maryland (Annapolis, 1946), pp. 89-90, 118.

like him from ever taking a seat in Parliament. The Maryland
government had adopted the same stance in 1716, disqualifying
from Assembly seats those who were ineligible to sit in Parliament.[23]  Thus when Hagar was elected to the Assembly in
1771, the matter of his eligibility was raised and the other
Assembly members voted to exclude him.[24]  However, a hastily
passed Maryland statute established eligibility for persons
in Hagar's situation.  Hagar was reelected and seated, barely
a month after the issue arose.[25]  A similar controversy crop-
ped up at the 1773 session of the Assembly and, after another
brief exclusion, Hagar was again permitted to participate.[26]
Hagar's success perfected the civil rights, in colonial Maryland, of the settlers who obtained Parliamentary naturalizations and established the opportunity for them to participate
fully in the life of their adopted land.

23 Archives of Maryland, XXX, p. 620.
24 Ibid., LXIII, pp. 90, 92, 93.
25 Ibid., LXIII, pp. 174, 238.
26 Ibid., LXIV, pp. 21-23.

EXPLANATORY NOTES

The format of the information derived from the different types of naturalization records which are presented in Parts I, II, and III has been kept as uniform as possible. The maximum amount of information which could be contained in each kind of line within a record is explained below in the same order used in the text. No original record is complete in all of these details.

Line type 1.　Identifying number of the record.
(In Part I a "D" and in Part II an "N" precedes the number. Entries in Part III have no alphabetical prefix.)

Date of naturalization or denization.

Date of communion (Part III only).

Source volume and page.
(The source of Parts I and II is the Maryland Archives. References in Part III are to Provincial Court Judgments libers on deposit at the Hall of Records.)

Line type 2.　Name of person naturalized or denizized.

County or town of residence.

Occupation.

City and/or nationality of origin.

Relationship to head of household.
(Parts I and II only.)

Church membership (Part III only).

"communion only," if named in communion certificate but failed to take qualifying oaths (Part III only).

Line type 3.  Denomination of communion service (Part III only).

Location of church or congregation in which communion administered (Part III only).

Line type 4.  Clergyman administering communion (Part III only).

Witnesses to communion (Part III only).

Within each record in this volume, the names of the naturalized have been arranged alphabetically, though families have been kept together as units.  Separate original records for which all items, except the data in the "type 2" lines, are identical have been combined into a single record.

All data in the denization records (Part I) were directly transcribed from the Maryland Archives volumes referenced.  Modern spellings of the names of counties were substituted for variant forms.

Part II is a composite of information from the Maryland Archives volumes and Bacon's Laws of Maryland.  The Archives' spellings were considered more reliable and were adopted here.  The naturalization date for each record was taken as the day the private act was signed into law.  Spellings of county names were modernized.

The naturalizations contained in Part III include all usable data from each original record.  Each of the original records in the Provincial Court Judgments libers begins with a list of those persons naturalized at that Court session.  Communion certificates, if recorded, follow, sometimes covering several folios.  An original record which includes communion certificates concludes with a second listing of those naturalized.

The folios cited in the references in this volume are those on which the first list of naturalized persons appears and not those of the communion certificates.  Spellings of names have been taken from the communion certificates, when available, to avoid the problems that English scribes sometimes experienced with non-English names.  Umlauts have been replaced by the original vowel followed by an "e".  In some cases, more likely spellings have been suggested for dis-

xiv

torted, but recognizable names. (Isagar and Wrightnomer are probably Hagar and Ridenaur.) A few names have been rearranged. (Tanner, Christian Getson and Backer, Bernard Wherton have become Getson Danner, Christian and Wherton Backer, Bernard.) The fondness of some of the clergy for latinized versions of names has not been tampered with. Persons named in the communion certificates, but not in the list of the naturalized, have been given "communion only" designations. Communion witnesses' names were transcribed as faithfully as possible. Occasionally, however, the combination of poorly written German script and the distortion of the recording process precluded interpretation. A single hyphen in a name represents an undecipherable letter; three hyphens indicate a partially illegible name.

Questionable or implied information is repeated as it appears in the original, but is enclosed in parentheses. (A location or date of a communion certificate signature, but not necessarily of communion administration is bracketed. Likewise, dates on records which fail to maintain the chronological order of their recording are indicated with parentheses.)

Place-names have been reproduced just as they were originally recorded. "Town" or "County" was copied for entries mentioning Frederick and Baltimore if that clarification was available. The religious denomination called Baptist here is the German Baptist sect now known as The Church of the Brethren. Although occasionally called Unitas Fratrum here, the Brethren should not be confused with the Moravians who also bear that Latin title. The locations of the communions administered by Church of England rectors are cited by parish name. Place-names, clergy, and parish locations are identified in the Appendix.

In using these records and indexes it should be remembered that in German names leading T's, B's, and K's are sometimes found as D's, P's, and C's, respectively, and vice versa. Family names beginning with an S followed by a consonant may begin as Sh or Sch followed by the consonant. Phonetic variations of German spellings frequently appear here. A signature as a witness, if available, most accurately portrays the immigrant's spelling of his name.

COLONIAL MARYLAND NATURALIZATIONS    PART I

DENIZATIONS GRANTED BY THE COUNCIL

D 1    January 14, 1660                                    MdA-3,398
Herman, Augustine            late of Manhatans, marchant

D 2    July 22, 1661                                       MdA-3,429
Meyor, Peter                 Swedish, late of New Amstel

D 3    July 29, 1661                                       MdA-3,429-430
Clementson, Andrew           Swedish, late of New Amstel
Cornelison, Mathias          Swedish, late of New Amstel
Harmer, Gothofrid            Swedish, late of New Amstel
Hendrickson, Batholomew      Swedish, late of New Amstel
Hendrickson, Hendrick        Swedish, late of New Amstel
Johnson, Paule               Swedish, late of New Amstel
Mathiason, Hendrick          Swedish, late of New Amstel
Micheelson, Clement          Swedish, late of New Amstel
Montson, Peter               Swedish, late of New Amstel
Sipherson, Marcus            Swedish, late of New Amstel
Stille, Axell                Swedish, late of New Amstel
Toreson, Andrew              Swedish, late of New Amstel
Urinson, Cornelius           Swedish, late of New Amstel
Urinson, John                Swedish, late of New Amstel
Wheeler, John                Swedish, late of New Amstel

D 4    July 30, 1661                                       MdA-3,430-431
Clauson, Jacob               Dutch, late of New Amstel
Comages, Cornelius           Dutch, late of New Amstel
Jarboe, John                 French
Micheelson, Jacob            Dutch, late of New Amstel
Vandernote, Michaell         Dutch, late of New Amstel

D 5    December 4, 1661                                    MdA-3,465
Brasseuir, Benojs            French, late of Virginia
  and his wife and children

D 6    January 23, 1662                                    MdA-3,466
Bedlo, Isaack                Dutch, late of England

D 7    February 17, 1662                                   MdA-3,470
Smith, Emperour              Dutch
Ubben, Barnard               Dutch

D 8     September 10, 1663                                    MdA-3,489
Lumbrozo, Jacob          alias John Lumbrozo, late of Lisbon Portugal

D 9     September 14, 1663                                    MdA-3,489
Lamore, Peter            of French descent
Lamore, Thomas           of French descent

D10     January 30, 1663/64                                  MdA-3,489
Sicks, Jno               German, late of England

D11     March 4, 1663/64                                     MdA-3,490
Pouston, John            subject of Scotland

D12     March 2, 1664/65                                     MdA-3,513
Le Compte, Antoine
 and his wife and children

D13     March 2, 1664/65                                     MdA-3,514
Ganison,Egbrett          of Petuxent
Guerin, Gasper
 and his heirs

D14     July 13, 1665                                        MdA-3,529
Fountaine, Nicholas      French, late of Virginia

D15     October 7, 1665                                      MdA-3,533
Marchegay, Bennitt       French

D16     Ocotber 12, 1666                                     MdA-3,557
Barbery, Thomas          Portuguese

D17     March 17, 1667                                       MdA-5,25
Martin, Abdelo
 and his children

D18     July 17, 1667                                        MdA-5,11
Jourdean, John

D19     February 26, 1668                                    MdA-5,35
Johnson, Hendrick        late of Amsterdam

D20     March 23, 1668                                       MdA-5,36
Mills, Peter             late of Holland

D21     April 19, 1669                                       MdA-5,37
Ticke, William           late of Amsterdam

D22    May 8, 1675                                        MdA-15,44
Stykelkan, Mense              Dutch

COLONIAL MARYLAND NATURALIZATIONS   PART II

NATURALIZATIONS GRANTED BY ENACTMENT OF PRIVATE LAWS

N 1    May 1, 1666                                        MdA-2,89
Neale, Anthony                children of Capt. James Neale and Anna, his
Neale, Dorothy                wife, who were born in Spain and Portugal
Neale, Henieretta Maria       while Neale served there
Neale, Janees

N 2    May 1, 1666                                       MdA-2,144
Hak, Anna                     born in Amsterdam, Holland
Hak, George                   son of Anna, born at Accomacke, Virginia
Hak, Peter                    son of Anna, born at Accomacke, Virginia
Herman, Augustine             born in Prag, Bohemia
Herman, Anna                  daughter of Augustine Herman
Herman, Casparus              son of Augustine Herman
Herman, Ephraim               son of Augustine Herman
Herman, Francina              daughter of Augustine Herman
Herman, Georgius              son of Augustine Herman
Herman, Judith                daughter of Augustine Herman
Herman, Margarita             daughter of Augustine Herman
Jarboe, John                  alias John Parks, of Dijon, France

N 3    May 8, 1669                                       MdA-2,205
DeBarrette, Isaac             born in Harlem, Holland
Dele Roche, Charles           French
Johnson, Peter                Swedish
Jourdain, Jean                born in Rouan, France
Roelands, Robert              born in Brabant, Holland
Van Heeck, John               born in Virginia
Vanswaringen, Garrett         born in Reensterdwan, Holland
DeBarette, Barbarah           born in Valenchene, in the Low Countries
                              when under Spanish control, wife of Garrett
Vanswaringen, Elizabeth       born in New Amstel, daughter of Garrett and
                              Barbarah
Vanswaringen, Zacharias       born in New Amstel, son of Garrett and
                              Barbarah

N 4    April 19, 1671                                    MdA-2,270
Besson, Stephen               of Dorchester County, French
Gottee, John                  of Dorchester County, French
Gottee, Margaret              of Dorchester County, wife of John, French
Johnson, Barnard              of Calvert County, Dutch
Nengfinger, William           of St. Mary's County, Dutch

N 5    April 19, 1671                                    MdA-2,282
Cartwright, Matthew           of St. Mary's County, born in Middlebourgh,
                              Province of Zealand
Cordea, Marke                 of St. Mary's County, born in Normandy
De Mouderer, Anthony          of Anne Arundel County, French
de Ring, Hans Jacob           of Baltimore County, Dutch
de Young, Jacob Clause        of Baltimore County, Dutch
Dhyniossa, Alexander          of Fosters Island, Talbot County, Dutch
Dhyniossa, Margaretta         wife of Alexander, of Talbot County, Dutch
Dhyniossa, Alexander          son of Alexander
Dhyniossa, Barbara            daughter of Alexander
Dhyniossa, Christina          daughter of Alexander
Dhyniossa, Johanna            daughter of Alexander
Dhyniossa, Johannes           son of Alexander
Dhyniossa, Maria              daughter of Alexander
Dhyniossa, Peter              son of Alexander
Elexson, John                 of Kent County, Swedish
Fontaine, Nicholas            of Somerset County, French
Garrets, Rutgertson           of Baltimore County, Dutch
Lederer, John                 of Calvert County, German
Mills, Peter                  of St. Mary's County, Dutch
Peterson, Mathias             of Talbot County, Dutch
Peterson, Peter               son of Mathias
Toulson, Andrew               of Baltimore County, Swedish
Turner, Thomas                of Anne Arundel County, born in Middlebourgh
                              Province of Zealand


N 6    October 20, 1671                                  MdA-2,330
De Costa, Mathias             of St. Mary's County, Portuguese


N 7    October 20, 1671                                  MdA-2,331
Comegys, Cornelius the elder  born in Lexmont, Holland
Comegys, Millementy           wife of Cornelius, born in Barnevelt,
                              Holland
Comegys, Cornelius the younger  born in Virginia
Comegys, Elizabeth            wife of Cornelius the younger
Comegys, Hannah               daughter of Cornelius the younger
Comegys, William              son of Cornelius the younger
Hansun, Hans                  born in Delaware Bay of Swedish parents


N 8    June 6, 1674                                      MdA-2,400
Anderson, Mounts              Swedish
Arenson, Cornelius            Dutch
Christian, Lawrence           German
Clements, Andrew              Swedish
Colke, Oliver                 Swedish
Cordea, Hester                born in Deepe, Normandy

| | |
|---|---|
| Desjardines, John | French |
| Enloes, Henry | Dutch |
| Freeman, Henry | Swedish |
| Henderson, Henry | Swedish |
| Jacobson, Jeffrey | Swedish |
| Johnson, Cornelius | born in Fiacina, Holland |
| Mugenbrough, Martin | German |
| Nomers, John | Swedish |
| Peterson, Cornelius | Swedish |
| Peterson, Hans | Danish |
| Lacounte, Anthony | children of Anthony Lacounte of Picardie, |
| Lacounte, Hester | France, who were born in Maryland |
| Lacounte, John | |
| Lacounte, Moses | |
| Lacounte, Phillip | |
| Lacounte, Katherine | |
| Lemaire, John | born in Anjou, France |
| Stille, Axell | Swedish |
| Syserson, Marcus | Swedish |
| Tick, William | born in Amsterdam, Holland |

N 9     June 6, 1674                                MdA-2,403
Green, Henry          of Talbot County, Dutch
Johnson, John         of Talbot County, Dutch

N10     February --, 1674                           MdA-2,460
Achilles, Peter       Spanish
Brispoe, Anthony      born in Amsterdam, Holland
Duhattoway, Jacob     born in Dort, Holland

N11     November 15, 1678                           MdA-7,78
Guibert, Joshua       born in Rheimes, France

N12     November 15, 1678                           MdA-7,79
Lookerman, Jacob      born in New York when under Dutch control
Peane, James          French
Peane, Magdelen       wife of James
Peane, Anne           daughter of James

N13     September 17, 1681                          MdA-7,216
Blangey, Lewis
Boys, Cornel
Fowcate, Peter
Ouldson, Peter

N14     May 13, 1682                                MdA-7,330

| Alward, John | of Charles County | |
| Erickson, Mathew | of Kent County | |
| Johnson, Albort | of Talbot County | |
| Looton, Jacob | of St. Mary's County | |

| N15    November 17, 1682 | | MdA-7,444 |
| Blankenstein, William | of St. Mary's County | |
| Nans, Rowld | of Baltimore County | |

| N16    November 6, 1683 | | MdA-7,487 |
| Anleton, Peter | | |
| Johnston, Simon | | |
| Peterson, Mathias | | |
| and his children | | |
| Poulson, Andrew | alias Mullock | |

| N17    November 16, 1683 | | MdA-7,461 |
| Cosins, John | | |
| Maise de Moise, Peter | | |
| Mattson, Andrew | | |

| N18    April 26, 1684 | | MdA-13,126 |
| Bayard, Peter | | |
| Daunces, Jasper | | |
| DeLaGrange, Arnoldus | | |
| Seth, Jacob | | |
| Sleyter, Peter | | |
| Verbrack, Nicholas | | |

| N19    November 19, 1686 | | MdA-13,144 |
| Berte, Paul | | |
| Berte, Mary | wife of Paul | |
| Brown, Derick | | |

| N20    June 9, 1692 | | MdA-13,536 |
| Ouldson, John | of Kent County | |
| Vanderheyden, Mathias | of Cecil County | |

| N21    March 1, 1694 | | MdA-19,137 |
| Dauison, Daniel Sr. | of Calvert County | |
| Dauison, Daniel Jr. | of Calvert County | |

| N22    October 18, 1694 | | MdA-19,103 |
| Ambrose, Abraham | | |
| Dee Koch Brune, Lewis | | |
| de la Montaigne, Nicholas | | |
| de Vagha, John | | |

Dutitree, Claudius
Ferdinando, Peter
 and his children
Imbert, Andrew
Missells, Gerardus
Missells, James                son of Gerardus
Sluiter, Jacob Jr.
Sluyter, Hendrick
van Burkelo, Herman


N23    May 22, 1695                            MdA-19,211
Camperson, Leonard
Golley, Peter                  of Talbot County
Goutee, John                   of Talbot County
Goutee, Joseph                 of Talbot County
Goutee, Joseph                 son of Joseph
Goutee, John                   son of Joseph
Mathiason, Mathias             alias Freeman, of Cecil County


N24    October 19, 1695                        MdA-19,281
Curtis, Michael                of St. Mary's County, Gentleman
Forbes, Alexander              of Talbot County
Steelman, John Hans            of Cecil County
Steelman, John Hans Jr.        of Cecil County


N25    May 14, 1696                            MdA-19,378
Edgar, John                    of Somerset County, Gentleman


N26    June 11, 1697                           MdA-19,596
Francis, Stephen               Italian
Sleycomb, George               German


N27    April 4, 1698                           MdA-22,148
Dowdee, Peter                  of Somerset County, French


N28    May 9, 1700                             MdA-24,107
Bellicane, Michael Sr.         of Cecil County, born of Dutch parents
Bellicane, Michael Jr.         of Cecil County, born of Dutch parents
Bellicane, Christopher         son of Michael Jr.
Bellicane, James               son of Michael Jr.
Mounts, Christopher            of Cecil County, born of Dutch parents


N29    May 17, 1701                            MdA-24,204
Debruler, John                 of Baltimore County
Debruler, John                 son of John
Debruler, William              son of John
  together with other sons and daughters born in this Province

Scamper, Peter                          of Prince George's County

N30    March 25, 1702                              MdA-24,279
Broord, James
Broord, James                  of Kent County, son of James
Broord, John                   of Kent County, son of James
Broord, Solomon                of Kent County, son of James
Collickman, Derrick            of Cecil County, of Dutch parents, planter
Oleg, Sebastian                of Anne Arundel County, German
Schee, Hermann                 of Cecil County, of Dutch parents, gentleman
Vanbiber, Isaac                of Cecil County, of Dutch parents, gentleman
Vanbiber, Mathias              of Cecil County, of Dutch parents, merchant

N31    May 3, 1704                                 MdA-24,410
Livers, Arnold                 taylor, Dutch
Smithers, Christopher          of Annapolis, taylor, German
Tawers, John                   of Cecil County, gentleman

N32    October 3, 1704                             MdA-26,366
Othason, Otho                  of Cecil Co., born in Pa. of Dutch parents

N33    May 25, 1705                                MdA-26,515
Dangerman, Christopher         of Calvert County, saddler, born in Hannover

N34    April 19, 1706                              MdA-26,620
Tyler, John Baptist            of Prince George's County, planter

N35    April 15, 1707                              MdA-27,152
Holland, John Francis          of Baltimore County, German

N36    December 17, 1708                           MdA-27,369
Defour, Benjamin               of Anne Arundel County, planter, French
Kitchin, Justus Englehard      painter, German
Robert, James                  of Calvert County, planter, French

N37    November 11, 1709                           MdA-27,481
Pacquett, Daniell              of Anne Arundel County, labourer

N38    November 4, 1710                            MdA-27,578
Swormstedt, Christian          of Calvert County, chyrurgeon, German

N39    November 3, 1711                            MdA-38,133
Pagett, David                  of Queen Anne's County, planter, French
Pagett, Maudlin                wife of David
Pagett, Eliza                  daughter of David
 and children yet unborn

N40    November 3, 1711                              MdA-38,143
Cody, William                of Charles County, taylor
 and his children
Rashoon, Stephen             of Talbot County, planter
 and his children
Sanders, Peter               of Talbot County, planter
 and his children

N41    November 15, 1712                             MdA-38,159
Guichard, Samuel             of Anne Arundel County, planter

N42    November 15, 1712                             MdA-38,165
Crismand, Joseph             of Charles County, planter
Nelson, Ambrose              of Baltimore County, planter
Overard, Peter               of Annapolis, saddler
Packett, David               of Anne Arundel County, labourer

N43    November 14, 1713                             MdA-38,181
Berry, Samuel                of Kent County, carpenter, Swedish
Larnee, John                 of Dorchester County, weaver
 and his children
Rich, Stephen                of Queen Anne County, carpenter
 and his children

N44    June 3, 1715                                  MdA-38,182
Harvey, Thomas               of Calvert County, French
 and his children

N45    April 22, 1720                                MdA-38,261
Kinkee, Herman               of Cecil County, Dutch
 and his children
Laviele, John                of Calvert County, French
Manadoe, Peter               of Cecil County, French
 and his children
Parandier, James             of Charles County, French
Parandier, John              of Charles County, French

N46    October 27, 1720                              MdA-38,277
Zenger, John Peter           of Kent County, printer, born in the Upper
 and his children            Palatinate on the Rhine

N47    August 5, 1721                                MdA-38,288
Geist, Christian             of Annapolis, gentleman, Swedish
Hesselius, Gustavus          of Prince George's County, limner, Swedish
Hesselius, Mary              daughter of Gustavus, born in Maryland
Lazear, Joseph               of Prince George's County, planter, German
Lazear, Deborah              daughter of Joseph, born in Maryland

Lazear, Elizabeth          daughter of Joseph, born in Maryland
Lazear, John               son of Joseph, born in Maryland
Lazear, Joseph             son of Joseph, born in Maryland
Lazear, Mary               daughter of Joseph, born in Maryland
Lazear, Thomas             son of Joseph, born in Maryland

N48     February 28, 1721/2                    MdA-38,297
Greening, Albert           of Anne Arundel County, German
 and his children
Oeth, John                 of Anne Arundel County, German
 and his children

N49     November 4, 1724                       MdA-38,346
Swineyard, John            of Baltimore County, planter, French

N50     November 6, 1725                       MdA-38,377
Ury, Michael               of Prince George's County, Greek
 and his children

N51     October 30, 1727                       MdA-38,403
Bodien, Francis Ludolph    of Kent County, chirurgeon, German
Bodien, Anne               daughter of Francis Ludolph
Bodien, Eliza              daughter of Francis Ludolph
Bodien, Hannah             daughter of Francis Ludolph
Bodien, Henry Augustus     son of Francis Ludolph
Bodien, Sophie Sidonia     daughter of Francis Ludolph

N52     October 30, 1727                       MdA-38,404
Maynadier, Rev. Daniel     of Talbot County, clerk, French
Maynadier, Daniel          son of Daniel
Maynadier, Jane            daughter of Daniel

N53     October 30, 1727                       MdA-38,406
Woolf, Garrett             of Annapolis, shoemaker
Woolf, John                of Annapolis, shoemaker
Woolf, Hannah              wife of John
Woolf, Annalesse           daughter of John
Woolf, Hanna               daughter of John
Woolf, Peter               son of John
Woolf, Maudlin             of Annapolis, spinster

N54     October 30, 1727                       MdA-38,407
Mynskie, John Samuel       of Annapolis, blacksmith, born in Branden-
                            burgh, Prussia
Mynskie, Catherine         wife of John Samuel
Mynskie, Susanah           daughter of John Samuel

N55     October 30, 1727                                    MdA-38,415
Montgomery, Peter               of Charles County, planter, French
Montgomery, Francis             son of Peter
Montgomery, John Baptista       son of Peter

N56     October 24, 1728                                    MdA-38,422
Rayman, William                 of Annapolis, German

N57     August 8, 1729                                      MdA-38,424
Peters, Christian               of Cecil County, German

N58     June 16, 1730                                       MdA-37,572
Hendrickson, John               of Kent County, native of Roterdam
Hendrickson, Hanah              daughter of John
Hendrickson, John               son of John
Hendrickson, Margaret           daughter of John
Hendrickson, Martha             daughter of John
Hendrickson, Mary               daughter of John
Hendrickson, Mildred            daughter of John
Hendrickson, Rachel             daughter of John
Hendrickson, Rebecca            daughter of John
Hendrickson, Ruth               daughter of John
Hendrickson, Samuel             son of John

N59     August 8, 1732                                      MdA-37,567
Rozilini, Onorio                of Annapolis, born in Venetian territories

N60     June 4, 1744                                        MdA-42,602
Richard, James                  of Baltimore County, born in Rochel, France

N61     April 24, 1762                                      MdA-58,206
Bouquet, Col. Henry
Victor, Frederick               of Annapolis, gentleman

N62     December --, 1769                                   MdA-62,120
Haldimand, Peter                gentleman

N63     November 20, 1771                                   MdA-63,281
Weisenthal, Charles Frederick
                                of Baltimore Town for more than 12 years,
                                physician, German, ordered to comply with
                                Statute 13 George II c.7

NATURALIZATIONS GRANTED UNDER STATUTES
13 GEORGE II c.7 AND 20 GEORGE II c.44


1    October 13, 1742                                    EI- 7,108
Spencer, Zachariah          German


2    October 15, 1742             October 10, 1742       EI- 7,110
Kince, Philip               German
Laney, Titus                German
Reislin, Matthew            German
  Lutheran Congregation at the church at Monockecey
  Stover          wit Joseph Jast Smith, John George Beyer


3    October 18, 1742             October 16, 1742       EI- 7,112
Harout, Peter                    of Charles County, native of France
  St. Anne's
  Lake          wit John Wilmott, Elinor King


4    October 18, 1742                                    EI- 7,112
Alforino, Phineas           a Jew


5    May 17, 1743                 April 10, 1743         EI- 7,161
House, John                 German
Kemp, Conrad                German
  Reformed, Monackese
  Rieger          wit Peter Hoffman, Heinrich -eupf


6    October 18, 1743             October 2, 1743        EI- 7,295
Fauz, Jacob                      of Cannawatke
Herriot, Andreas                 of Cannawatke
Kinzmiller, Martin               of Cannawatke
  in the Lutheran Church at Cannewatke
  Chandler


7    October 19, 1743             September 25, 1743     EI- 7,296
Ambrose, Mateas                  of Manaquice
Heyell, John George              of Manaquice
Huzel, John George               of Manaquice
Scheidler, George                of Manaquice
Sweinhart, George                of Manaquice
Verdris, Valentine               of Manaquice
Wezler, Martain                  of Manaquice
  in the Lutheran Church at Manaquice
  Chandler        wit Philip Kince, John Shrier

8     October 19, 1743          June 26, 1743          EI- 7,296
Verdress, John
 in the Lutheran Church at Manaquice
 Chandler        wit John George Bear, Mathias Reislin

9     October 19, 1743          October 18, 1743          EI- 7,296
Erhard, Conrad
Middlecave, Peter
Pickler, Mark
Shrier, George
Shrier, Jacob
Shrier, John
Shrier, Nicholas
Shriver, Andrew
Shriver, Lutwick
Will, Michael
Young, David
 St. Anne's
 Jenings        wit Garret Woolfe, Thos King

10     October 19, 1743          October 9, 1743          EI- 7,296
Boughtall, Henry
Hend, John
Miller, Isaac
Mire, Gasper
Staley, Jacob
Stall, Adam
Stern, Jacob
Getson Tanner, Christian
 Templeman        wit Jacob Runner, John Peter Houghman

11     October 19, 1743                              EI- 7,297
Knave, Jaed                     a Quaker
Shope, Martain                  a Quaker

12     October 27, 1743          October 26, 1743          EI- 7,302
Gash, Conjuist
Gash, Godfrey
 St. Anne's
 Bourdillon     wit John Willmott, Elinor King

13     April 10, 1746          April 9, 1746          EI-10,44
Gump, George                    of Prince George's County
 St. Anne's
 Gordon         wit Katherine Minskie, Gabriel Fisher

14     September 27, 1746                          EI-10,228

Hoofman, Peter
Kemp, Christian
Kemp, Gilbert

15    October (20), 1747                        EI-10,657
Avey, Henry
French, George
Gratt, Felta                a Quaker
Hobre, Andrew
Isagar, Jonathan            Jonathan Hagar
Keisner, Martain
Miller, Jacob
Miller, Lodowick
Rorrer, Jacob
Simmons, Isaac
Stull, Jacob
Vulgamot, Joseph
Wrightnomer, Nicholas       Nicholas Ridenaur

16    April 26, 1750                            EI-13,7
Barnets, Daniel
Hartway, Feiters

17    September 26, 1750                         EI-13,207
Myar, Peter

18    September 16, 1751                         EI-13,801
Hoffman, John
Kemp, Frederick

19    September 17, 1751                         EI-13,803
Bertnitz, Carl
Hartman, George
Israollo, Angel
Meyerer, Michael
Shmith, Cannerah
Sommer, John

20    September 29, 1752                         EI-14,568
Clont, Jacob
Cuikes, Hendrick
Myer, Valentine

21    April 11, 1753                            EI-14,778
Hagmayre, Conrode
Ridenaur, Henry
Ridenaur, Matthias

Ridenaur, Peter
Winteroth, Casparus

22     September 12, 1753                  EI-15,155
Burkitt, George
Burkitt, Matthias
Hartsman, Mathias Ulrich
Ruff, Michael
Wild, Jacob

23     September 14, 1753                  EI-15,157
Fierst, Martin
Honey, George
Hoofman, John

24     September 24, 1753                  EI-15,160
Hansith, Bernhard Michael
Hariman, Joseph

25     September 25, 1753                  EI-15,161
Lazyrus, Henry          a Jew

26     May 19, 1756                       BT- 1,4
Eshpaw, John
Hoolf, Jacob

27     May 21, 1756                       BT- 1,6
Smith, Casper

28     October 21, 1756       October 17, 1756     BT- 1,274
Priggs, John               of Prince George's County, German
St. Paul's
Eversfeild

29     October 25, 1756       August 13, 1756      BT- 1,274
Greenevald, Philip        German
Fux, George              German
Misler, Ulrich          German
Reformed
Stoner       wit Valentine Maurer, John Dilbone

30     August 31, 1757        July 20, 1757       BT- 2,4
Decker, Rudolph
Shilling, Jacob Sr.
Shreider, William
Reformed (York)
Lischy       wit Milchor Kiner, Frantz Noll

31      August 31, 1757          August 7, 1757          BT- 2,4
Baum, George Peter              communion only
Baum, Simon                     communion only
Born, Michael
Horch, Elias                    communion only
Mengen, Peter
Utz, Jacob
 Lutheran (Mannsl Township)
 Bager          wit Jean de Grange, Ullrich Eggler

32      August 31, 1757          (August 21, 1757)        BT- 2,4
Noll, Antonius
Schlothaver, Nicholas
 Lutheran (Canawage)
 Bager

33      August 31, 1757          August 1, 1757          BT- 2,4
Ecklor, Ulrick
Gettier, Christopher
 Reformed (Manheim Township)
 Lischy          wit Jos. Peter Meuyin, Malichar Kiner

34      August 31, 1757          August 8, 1757          BT- 2,4
Edleman, Philip
 Reformed (Baltimore County)
 Lischy

35      September 1, 1757        August 31, 1757          BT- 2,6
Shilling, Jacob Jr.
Stofel, Henry
 Church of England
 Brooke

36      April 12, 1758           March 3, 1758          BT- 3,270
Coop, Nichlaus                  communion only
Dieter, Theobald
Hahn, Lodowich
Wagener, Michael                communion only
 Lutheran (York)
 Bager          wit Henrich Schlegel, Johann Friedrich Gall, Johann ---
                wit Andreas Scheever, Johannes Bischoff

37      April 12, 1758           March 16, 1758          BT- 3,270
Rheinhard, Valentin             of Mannheim Twp. near the Maryland border
 (Conawago)
 Bager          wit Hans Jarg Keller, Milcher Kinner

38      April 17, 1758           March 26, 1758          BT- 3,284
Lingenfelter, Abraham        living in Frederick Town
Reformed, Frederick Town
Steiner        wit Thomas Schley, Henrick Shover, Johannes Gomber


39      September 13, 1758       (September 11, 1758)    BT- 3,558
Harts, John
Kipports, Jacob
Pfeiffer, Henrick
Shloy, John                  communion only
Stamber, Christopher
Stiger, Andreas
Ulrich, Peter
 Reformed (Baltimore)
Lischy          wit Jacob Mayer, Valentine Larsch


40      September 13, 1758       (August 20, 1758)      BT- 3,558
Zimmerman, Sebastian         Bedepscko habitans
 (Baltimore Town)
Kirchner


41      September 13, 1758       (August 8, 1758)       BT- 3,558
Gallman, Jacob               Alsatian
 Lutheran (Frederick Town)
Hausihl         wit Michael Stumpf, Carl Schell, Veltir Swartz


42      September 13, 1758       (September 9, 1758)     BT- 3,558
Lingenfelter, Johannes
 Reformed (Frederick Town)
Steiner         wit Thomas Schley


43      September 15, 1758       (August 12, 1758)      BT- 3,562
Tuchmannus, Peter            8 years away from Alsace
 Lutheran (Frederick Town)
Hausihl


44      September 15, 1758       within past 3 months   BT- 3,562
Valentine, George            Francus, 7 years away from Germany
Wolf, Hendrick               from Hundsbach ad Rhinum
 Lutheran (Frederick Town), members at Hunting Creek
Hausihl


45      September 23, 1758       (August 19, 1758)      BT- 3,569
Groes, Philippus
 Lutheran (York)
Bager

46      April 11, 1759          March 4, 1759          BT- 3,868
Baum, George Simon
Gummell, Martinus
Horch, Johannes Elias
Mathias, Stephan
Welty, Andrew                   communion only
  Lutheran (York)
  Bager          wit Jorg Simon Baum, Peter Welty

47      April 11, 1759          April 1, 1759          BT- 3,868
Fliegel, Valentine
Gor, Michael
Haberte, John                   communion only
Kraeuter, John
Neef, Henrich                   communion only
Pflubach, Jacob
Roster, John
Runchel, Joest                  communion only
Ulrich, Matheus
Zacharias, Daniel               communion only
  Reformed (Frederick County)
  Lischy         wit Vallendin Meiurs, Johan Martin Kutzmueller

48      April 11, 1759                                 BT- 3,868
Meyer, Friedrich                communion only
Shloy, John
Stigar, Andrew
  Reformed
  Lischy         wit Morice Werseler, Henry Walter

49      April 12, 1759          December 25, 1758      BT- 3,870
Warner, Nicholas                a member
  Reformed, Friderix Town
  Steiner         wit John Weller, Jacob Scheren

50      April 12, 1759          March 4, 1759          BT- 3,870
Welty, Andrew                   same certificate as in 46, rerecorded
  Lutheran (York)
  Bager          wit Jorg Simon Baum, Peter Welty

51      April 12, 1759          April 7, 1759          BT- 3,871
Protzman, Lawrence              of Frederick County, potter
  Moravian, Frederickstown County
  Zahm           wit Samuel Herr, Leonhard Moser

52      April 17, 1759          April 15, 1759         BT- 3,876
Thomas, John

Thomas, Valentine
Woolf, Adam
 Reformed, Frederick Town
 Steiner          wit Johann Gomber, Georg Hoffman, Thomas Schley


53     July 18, 1759          April 15, 1759          BT- 3,886
Come, Adam
Kassler, Barnard
Shissler, Adam
Tofelor, Peter
 Reformed, Frederick Town
 Stiner          wit Johannes Gomber, Heinrich Schaber


54     September 12, 1759      August 27, 1759        BT- 5,208
Biegler, Heinrick
Biess, Henrich           communion only
Brecht, Wentel
Brost, Conrod
Eberhard, Paul           communion only
Feder, Henrich
Kessler, Jacob           communion only
Libby, Conrod            communion only
Lictich, Peter           communion only
Reinhard, Georg          communion only
Shaura, John
 Reformed (Baltimore)
 Lischy          wit Jacob Myer, Daniel Bower


55     September 12, 1759      (August 5, 1759)       BT- 5,208
Allgeyer, Johannes
Heppenheimer, Andrew
 (Baltimore Town)
 Kirchner        wit Adam Gough, Andrew Caum


56     September 12, 1759      August 26, 1759        BT- 5,208
Joon, Jochem
Meyer, Frederick
 Reformed
 Lischy          wit Morice Wersler, John Holer


57     September 12, 1759      September 2, 1759       BT- 5,208
Erb, Peter
 Lischy          wit (Phib Colmann), Peter ---


58     September 12, 1759      (September 7, 1759)     BT- 5,208
Hahn, Michael                   a member
 Lutheran (Canewage)

Bager          wit Johannes Sheu-es, Conrad Bruegh

59    September 12, 1759                              BT- 5,208
Kraemer, Peter
(Baltimore County)
Kirchner       wit Martine Teusch, Johannes Kirbel

60    September 12, 1759      September 4, 1759      BT- 5,208
Kneegher, Michael            of Frederick County
Lutheran Congregation on Catocting
Shlees         wit Peter Beaver, George Soldner

61    September 12, 1759      (August 7, 1759)      BT- 5,208
Lautenschlaeger, Philip
Ruebel, Johannes
(Baltimore County)
Kirchner       wit Martin Teusch, Petter Littich

62    September 12, 1759      (August 5, 1759)      BT- 5,208
Faul, Johannes               Baltimore Town inhabitant
Gantz, Adam                  Baltimore Town inhabitant
Reichart, Jacob              Baltimore Town inhabitant  communion only
Tiefenbach, Michael          Baltimore Town inhabitant, communion only
(Baltimore Town)
Kirchner       wit Morice Wersler, Will Hackel

63    April 9, 1760           (March 2, 1760)       BT- 5,509
Braun, Georg Frederick       Baltimore Town inhabitant
Conradi, Conrad              Baltimore Town inhabitant
Dieffenbach, Michael         Baltimore Town inhabitant
Littich, Peter               Baltimore Town inhabitant
Rack, Georg Jacob            Baltimore Town inhabitant
Theil, Philipp               Baltimore Town inhabitant, communion only
Werseheler, Mauritius        Baltimore Town inhabitant
(Baltimore Town)
Kirchner       wit Valentine Larsch, Frederick Meyer, Jacob Richbortz
               wit Jacob Mayer

64    April 9, 1760           March 23, 1760        BT- 5,509
Dornbach, Christoffell       of Baltimore County
Ibach, Jacob                 of Baltimore County
Meyer, Georg                 of Baltimore County
Schmare, Martin              of Baltimore County
Slagel, Ernst                of Baltimore County
Reformed, Baltimore
Lischy         wit Valentine Larsch, Jacob Richbortz

65     April 10, 1760            April 6, 1760              BT- 5,510
Bagenpok, Casper                 of Frederick County
Cristen, Jacob                   of Frederick County
Cronice, George                  of Frederick County
Dearner, Jacob                   of Frederick County
Everly, Adam                     of Frederick County
Everly, Linnard                  of Frederick County
Fluck, Jacob                     of Frederick County
Herbogh, Ludvik                  of Frederick County
Kile, Adam                       of Frederick County
Wiliard, Theobald                of Frederick County
Reformed, Congregation in Kittockting Mountains
Bower          wit Lenert Ewerle, Philipp Carl Haass


66     April 10, 1760            January 26, 1760          BT- 5,510
Kifaber, Philip
Letterman     wit Bartholomew Cuger, Georg Sheitler


67     April 11, 1760            April 3, 1760             BT- 5,512
Aberlae, John
Neaf, Henrick
Ronckel, Jost
Zacharias, Daniel               communion only
Reformed, Manheim Township in York County
Lischy         wit Adam Hubert, Petter Stumell


68     April 14, 1760            April 6, 1760             BT- 5,513
Bitzell, Henry
Pinckly, John              John Binckly
Reformed, Congregation in Kettockting Mountains
Bower          wit Lenert Ewerly, Philipp Carl Haass


69     April 14, 1760            February 3, 1760          BT- 5,513
Leaderman, Michael         German
Link, Andrew               German
Reformed, Frederick County
Stonner        wit Johannes Plenner, Johannes Keller


70     April 16, 1760            April 13, 1760            BT- 5,514
Back, Balthasar            of the town of Frederick near Manakoese
Schell, Carle              of the town of Frederick near Manakoese
Weis, Henrick              of the town of Frederick, communion only
Lutheran, Manakoese
Bager          wit Jacob Beyr, Conrod Grosh, Michael Romer


71     April 16, 1760            January 20, 1760          BT- 5,514
Clem, George

Whitman, Frederick
Shmidt          wit Jacob Bech Shmidt, Feling Sautter

72    April 16, 1760          April 13, 1760          BT- 5,514
Tannwolf, Jacob Frederick     of the town of Frederick near Manrepe
Lutheran
Bager           wit Conrod Grosh, Balthasar Bach, Michael Romer
                wit Jacob Beyer

73    April 17, 1760                                  BT- 5,515
Dern, William

74    April 18, 1760          April 17, 1760          BT- 5,516
Shideacre, Valentine
Summer, Valentine
St. Anne's
Williamson    wit William Dern, Elizabeth Diller

75    September 10, 1760      (August 24, 1760)       BT- 5,806
Levely, William
(Baltimore County)
Kirchner      wit Philip Schnel, Herrath Cott

76    September 10, 1760      September 8, 1760        BT- 5,806
Pott, Conrod
Toil, Philip
Church of England
Chase         wit Willhelm Loeble, Adam Schoeck

77    September 10, 1760      (August 26, 1760)       BT- 5,806
Bernauer, Jacob
Born, Adam
Born, Georg
Gentz, Peter
Sneider, Jacob
Woerbel, Johannes Sr.
Woerbel, Johannes Jr.
 (Baltimore County)
Kirchner      wit Adam Geogh, Ernst Schlegel

78    September 10, 1760      (August 24, 1760)       BT- 5,806
Bayer, Melchior               communion only
Gaag, Adam
Kis, Friederich               communion only
 (Baltimore County)
Kirchner      wit Adam Schoeck, Philib Shnel

79      September 10, 1760        (August 24, 1760)        BT- 5,806
Schoeck, Adam
(Baltimore County)
Kirchner      wit Philip Shnel, Adam Gough

80      September 10, 1760        September 7, 1760        BT- 5,807
Irish, Francis                   Francis Frish
St. Thomas's
Craddock      wit Adam Schock, Ernst Schlegel

81      September 10, 1760        (September 10, 1760)     BT- 5,806
Reis, Henry
Wagoner, Michael
Weis, Adam
St. Anne's
Williamson      wit Adam Schock, Jacob Kleist

82      September 10, 1760        (August 24, 1760)        BT- 5,806
Dreish, Jacob
(Baltimore County)
Kirchner      wit Martin Teusch, Phillip Lauterschleger, Johannes Kiebel

83      September 10, 1760        July 27, 1760            BT- 5,806
Danner, Dieter
Goerts, Hartman
Rauh, Jacob                      communion only
Shindledeker, Jacob
Striker, Michael
Unger, Henry                     communion only
 our Congregation at Thomas Creek
Bager      wit Johan Georg Schmidt, Conrad Hakeshmitt

84      September 10, 1760        September 4, 1760        BT- 5,806
Bancker, Jacob
Danner, Jacob                    communion only
Rees, Adam
Zacharias, Daniel
 Reformed, Frederick County
Lischy      wit Peter Erb, Jost Runckel

85      September 10, 1760        (August 24, 1760)        BT- 5,808
Fraeger, Johann Georg            communion only
Lauteman, Johann Georg
Schnepf, Johann Peter            communion only
(Baltimore County)
Kirchner      wit Martin Teusch, Phillip Lauterschleger, Johannes Kiebel

86      September 11, 1760        June 22, 1760           BT- 5,808
Barr, George                     communion only
Buke, Matthew                    communion only
Dick, Conrad                     communion only
Eighenbrod, Jost
Hekman, Conrad
Huffman, George                  communion only
Reformed, Frederick Town
Otterbein      wit Henrich Shaber, Thomas Schley, Johannes Gomber
               wit Johannes Bruner


87      September 11, 1760                                BT- 5,809
Funk, Michael                    of Frederick County, German, a member
Rorer, Frederick                 of Frederick County, German, a member
Menonists


88      April 4, 1761            March 29, 1761          BT- 5,810
Keller, Jacob
Reformed (Frederick Town)
Otterbein      wit Henrich Shaber, Johannes Gomber


89      April 4, 1761            April 3, 1761           BT- 5,810
Garretson, Frederick             of Frederick County
Laeter, Malachi                  of Frederick County
Smith, Philip                    of Frederick County, communion only
St. Anne's
Keene         wit Conrad Merkell, Abraham Lingenfelder


90      April 4, 1761            April 4, 1761           BT- 5,810
Miller, Simon                    of Frederick County
St. Anne's
Keene         wit Conrad Merkell, Lud Righan


91      April 11, 1761           (April 8, 1761)         BT- 5,814
Shover, Henry                    of Frederick County, an elder of the Reform-
                                 ed Congregation in Frederick Town
Reformed, Frederick Town
Otterbein      wit Stephan Remesperger, Thomas Schley


92      April 11, 1761           March 29, 1761          BT- 5,814
Gomber, John
Weber, John
Reformed (Frederick Town)
Otterbein      wit Henrich Shober, Georg Hoffman


93      April 11, 1761           March 29, 1761          BT- 5,814
Schaaf, Casper

Reformed, Frederick Town
Otterbein        wit Henrich Schober, Thomas Schley, Johannes Bruner
                 wit Johannes Gomber

94      April 13, 1761              April 12, 1761             BT- 5,815
Apple Christian
Balchermire, Henry
Craismig, Jasper
Lob, Jacob
Shrim, John
Church of England (Baltimore County)
Chase          wit Maurice Wersler, Jacob Mayer, Friederich Meyer

95      April 13, 1761              March 29, 1761             BT- 5,815
Kost, Francis
Reformed, Frederick Town
Otterbein        wit Johannes Gomber, Henrich Schober, Thomas Schley

96      April 13, 1761              March 22, 1761             BT- 5,815
Merckell, Conrod                   of Annapolis, baker
St. Anne's
Keene          wit Chas. Bryan, John Fullford

97      April 13, 1761              March 22, 1761             BT- 5,815
Spease, Conrod                     of Frederick County
Reformed, Church at Catacter Mountain
Bauer          wit Ernst Ewerle, Andreiss Gerrard

98      April 13, 1761              March 22, 1761             BT- 5,815
Ostertoghr, Christian
Lutherian Congregation on Killockting
Schlets        wit Conrad Young, Peter Bever

99      April 13, 1761                                        BT- 5,816
Smith, Philip                  refers to certificate in 89

100     April 14, 1761              March 29, 1761             BT- 5,817
Holtz, Benedict
Reformed, Frederick Town
Otterbein        wit Thomas Schley, Jacob Henneger

101     April 14, 1761              March 29, 1761             BT- 5,817
Remschberger, Stephan              of Frederick County
Reformed (Frederick Town)
Otterbein        wit Johannes Gomber, Henrich Schaber

102     April 14, 1761              March 29, 1761             BT- 5,817

Madis, Daniel
Getsedaner, Gabriel
Remespergher, George
 Reformed, Frederick Town
 Otterbein       wit Stephan Remesperger, Thomas Schley

103    April 14, 1761              March 29, 1761          BT- 5,817
Beker, Samuel
 Reformed, Frederick Town
 Otterbein       wit Thomas Schley, Georg Hoffman

104    April 14, 1761              April 12, 1761          BT- 5,817
Hafner, Frederick              a member
 Lutheran, Frederick Town
 Gerock          wit Baltis Bough, Conrad Grosh

105    April 15, 1761              April 14, 1761          DD- 1,184
Lingenfelter, George
Storme, Vansel
 St. Anne's
 Keene           wit Conrod Merkell, Febb Greenwald

106    April 15, 1761              March 29, 1761          DD- 1,184
Folwyter, Henry
 Reformed, Frederick Town
 Otterbein       wit Johannes Gomber, Henrich Shober, Thomas Schley

107    April 15, 1761              April 12, 1761          DD- 1,184
Barth, Peter                  a member
Eder, Casper                  a member
Jesseroon, Michael            a member
Kruger, Casper                a member
Lenck, Adam                   a member
Sydeman, Jacob                a member
Vogel, Andrew                 a member
 Lutheran, Frederick Town
 Gerock          wit Conrod Grosh, Jacob Brys, Baltis Bough

108    April 15, 1761              April 12, 1761          DD- 1,184
Gibbs, Abraham
Hout, George
Missel, Frederick
Shott, Christian
 Frederick Town
 Geroch          wit Conrod Grosh, Jacob Brys, Baltis Bough

109    April 15, 1761              April 12, 1761          DD- 1,184

Troutman, Leonard            a member
Turner, George               a member
 Frederick Town
 Gerock          wit Conrad Grosh, Michael Romer


110    April 15, 1761                                 DD- 1,184
Gernhart, Henry              a member
 Gerock          wit Conrod Grosh, Michael Romirr


111    April 15, 1761            March 22, 1761       DD- 1,184
Gack, Philip
Goller, Jacob
Heckendoon, Jacob            communion only
Mossnerr, Dieterich
 Lutherian Church on the mittel end of Thames Creek
 Beck            wit Conrod Hackenschmid, John Herman Goertz
                 wit Deterich Danner


112    April 15, 1761            March 22, 1761       DD- 1,184
Acer, Adam
Polsell, Peter
 Reformed, Congregation at Kotocter
 Bauer           wit Jacob Young, Henrich Altman Jr., Valtin Med--


113    April 15, 1761            March 29, 1761       DD- 1,184
Froshaur, John
 Reformed, Frederick Town
 Otterbein       wit Thomas Schley, Jerg Hoffman


114    April 15, 1761            March 29, 1761       DD- 1,184
Goodman, William
 Reformed, Frederick Town
 Otterbein       wit Thomas Schley, Georg Hoffman


115    April 15, 1761            March 29, 1761       DD- 1,184
Darr, Sebastian
Marts, Theobald
Sheafer, Peter
Sumer, John
 Reformed, Frederick Town
 Otterbein       wit Stephan Remsperger, Thomas Schley


116    April 15, 1761            April 12, 1761       DD- 1,184
Alex, Michael                a member
Bayer, Jacob                 a member
Ebert, Adam                  a member
Foutin, Ann Mary             a member

Need, Matthias            a member
Wyghel, Adam
 Frederick Town
 Gerock        wit Conrod Grosh, Baltis Bough

117    April 15, 1761         March 29, 1761         DD- 1,184
Honerkin, Jacob
 Reformed, Frederick Town
 Otterbein    wit Jos Bendick Folt, Thomas Schley

118    April 15, 1761                                DD- 1,188
Weller, Jacob             German
 Minonist

119    April 16, 1761         March 22, 1761         DD- 1,189
Young, Jacob              of Frederick County
 All Saints'
 Bacon        wit John Kimbol, William Kimbol

120    April 16, 1761         March 29, 1761         DD- 1,189
Dick, Peter
 Reformed (Frederick Town)
 Otterbein    wit Stephan Remesperger, Thomas Schley

121    April 16, 1761         April 12, 1761         DD- 1,189
Gartenhower, Jacob
Spengler, Mathias
Shellman, John            a member
 Frederick Town
 Gerock       wit Conrod Grosh, Michael Romer

122    April 16, 1761         April 12, 1761         DD- 1,189
Sholl, Christian          a member
 Frederick Town
 Gerock       wit Conrod Grosh, Michael Schimpf, Jacob Brys

123    April 16, 1761         April 12, 1761         DD- 1,189
Hofman, Leonard           a member
 Lutheran
 Gerock       wit Conrod Grosh, Michael Romar

124    April 16, 1761         July 13, 1760          DD- 1,189
Wise, Henry
Gibbs, Abraham
Haut, John George
 Lutheran, Frederick Town
 Bager        wit Conrod Grosh, Michael Romar

125     April 16, 1761          March 29, 1761          DD- 1,189
Philips, Nicholas
Lutherian Congregation in Conigochegue
Schlets          wit John Boghner, Reinhard Walekenbough, Benedict Bowman

126     April 17, 1761          March 22, 1761          DD- 1,193
Bort, Nicholas
Lutheran, Congregation of Conigochigue
Schlets          wit John Schloss, Andreas Schloss

127     April 17, 1761          March 29, 1761          DD- 1,193
Barr, George
Reformed, Frederick Town
Otterbein          wit Thomas Schley, Michael Jesseroony

128     April 17, 1761          March 22, 1761          DD- 1,193
Schloss, Andreas
Lutheran, Congregation of Canawagen in York County
Bager          wit Jacob Stagle, (Hauving Bridonger)

129     September 9, 1761          May 23, 1761          DD- 1,488
Mosser, Leonard          of Frederick County, farmer and weaver
Moravian, Frederick County
Zahm          wit Lorentz Kriega, Frantz Prozmann, Georg Hendley

130     September 19, 1761          (August 9, 1761)          DD- 1,488
Allgayer, Jacob
Dike, Philip
Schnepf, Johannes Peter
(Baltimore County)
Kirchner          wit Adam Shaur, Phillip ---, Thomas Hooker

131     September 9, 1761          April 30, 1761          DD- 1,488
Jung, Johannes          a member
Canewake
Waldschmitt     wit David Shriver, Andrew Shriver, Augustus ---

132     September 9, 1761          August 23, 1761          DD- 1,488
Wottering, John Daniel          of Frederick County, farmer and carpenter
Moravian (Frederick County)
Zahn          wit Lorentz Krieger, George Gump

133     September 9, 1761          August 23, 1761          DD- 1,488
Heerback, John George          of Frederick County, farmer and joiner
Moravian, Frederick County
Zahn          wit Lorentz Prozmann, Lorentz Krieger, Leonhart Mosser

134     September 9, 1761          12 post Trinitatis      DD- 1,488
Baum, George Peter
Gro, Michael
Sabee, Leonhard                   communion only
Zebb, Peter
  Lutheran
  Bager          wit Johann Scheibel, George ---, --- Lentz

135     September 9, 1761          September 4, 1761       DD- 1,488
Ambros, Jacob
Hackerschmid, Conrad              an elder in his church
Rau, Andreas
Schmid, Georg
Ungerer, Henrick
  Lutheran, Mittee Creek
  Beck           wit Johan Hermer Goertz, Jacob Mathew, Dieterick Damer

136     September 9, 1761          August 23, 1761        DD- 1,488
Kreiger, Lorenz                   of Frederick County in Manakosy, farmer
  Moravian, Frederick County
  Zahn           wit Jacob Weller, Jan James Woettring, George Gump

137     September 9, 1761          August 30, 1761        DD- 1,488
Weller, Jacob                     a member
  Reformed, Canewake
  Waldschmidt    wit David Shriver, Andrew Shriver, Augustus Schoen

138     September 9, 1761          August 16, 1761        DD- 1,488
Feitt, Henrick
  Reformed (Catores, York County)
  Lischy         wit Devalt, Shneider, Daniel Zapf

139     September 9, 1761          August 16, 1761        DD- 1,488
Becker, Philip
Decker, Christopher Jr.
Fiet, Ulrick                      communion only
Houbman, Jacob                    communion only
Weinert, Nich                     communion only
  Manheim Townshipp, York County
  Lischy         wit Adam ---, Rudolf Decker

140     September 9, 1761          September 6, 1761       DD- 1,488
Schwartz, Valentine               of Frederick County
  All Saints'
  Bacon          wit Johan Georg Schmidt, Conrad ---

141     September 9, 1761          September 6, 1761       DD- 1,488

Huntz, Devalt                of Frederick County
Smidt, Jacob                 of Frederick County
Smidt, George                of Frederick County
 All Saints'
 Bacon           wit Valentin Schwartz, Johan Georg Schmidt

142    September 9, 1761          September 5, 1761       DD- 1,488
Danbach, Frederick
 Church of England, Baltimore
 Chase           wit Valentine Laudenberger, Michael Bainel

143    September 9, 1761          September 6, 1761       DD- 1,488
Leikteter, Conrad            of Frederick County
 All Saints'
 Bacon           wit Phaltine Schwartz, Jacob Schempf

144    September 9, 1761          September 8, 1761       DD- 1,488
Hadlar, Sebastian            of Anne Arundel County
Hammond, Andrew              of Anne Arundel County
Hammond, John George         of Anne Arundel County
Hammond, Mathew              of Anne Arundel County
Hemstone, Mathias            of Frederick County
Philpock, John               of Anne Arundel County
Rind, John                   of Anne Arundel County
Hammond, John                of Anne Arundel County
 St. Anne's
 Keene           wit Charles Bryan, Henery ---, Johan Peter Schnepf

145    September 9, 1761          August 9, 1761         DD- 1,488
Lattenburgher, Valentine
Pence, Michael
 St. Anne's
 Williamson      wit Conrod Morshall, Frederick ---

146    September 9, 1761          July 26, 1761          DD- 1,488
Brubecker, Rudulphus         a member
 Reformed, Canewake
 Waldschmidt     wit Auguste ---

147    September 9, 1761          September 9, 1761      DD- 1,488
Engle, Charles               of Frederick County
Eynklan, John                of Frederick County
Heuster, Francis             of Baltimore County
Hysson, Paulser              of Frederick County
Tryer, Frederick             of Frederick County
 St. Anne's
 Keene

148      September 10, 1761         July 13, 1761          DD- 1,495
Baney, Jacob
Fucks, John George
Michael, William
Wiggell, John
 Lutheran, Frederick Town
 Bager           wit Conrad Grosh, Baltis Bough


149      September 15, 1761         September 14, 1761     DD- 1,497
Puchie, Mathias                     of Frederick County
Shneider, Conrad                    of Frederick County
Shneider, Michael                   of Frederick County
Turney, John                        of Frederick County
Winter, Martin                      of Baltimore County
 St. Anne's
 Keene           wit Conrad Merkell, Jacob Sim


150      September 26, 1761         September 6, 1761      DD- 1,503
Roadrok, Andrew
 Congregation of the Dunkers
 Rooland         wit Anthony Hardman, Jacob Domer


151      April 14, 1762            April 4, 1762           DD- 2,87
Kibler, Michael                     of Frederick County, German, a member
 Lutheran, York County
 Bager           wit Yost Wagner, Johan Hoffley, Christian Unsreck


152      April 14, 1762            April 8, 1762           DD- 2,87
Grim, Andrew                        of Frederick County, German, a member
 at Antieatam Furnace Lutheran Congregation
 Shletz          wit Gerg Mikel Hang, Jacob Sandeker


153      April 14, 1762            March 24, 1762          DD- 2,87
Dietz, Michael                      German
Dilli, Johann                       German
Smidt, Carl                         German
 Baltimore County
 Kirchner        wit Michael Born, Anthoni Noll


154      April 14, 1762            March 21, 1762          DD- 2,87
Beyer, Melchior                     German, communion only
Leinberger, Andreas                 German
Zimmerman, George                   German, communion only
 Baltimore County
 Kirchner        wit Johannes Allgier, Jacob Collyday


155      April 14, 1762            April 4, 1762           DD- 2,87

Diel, Nicholas              German
Hool, Andreas              German, communion only
Meyer, John               German
Steinstaeuffer, Daniel         German
Stoude, Martin             German
Shawn, Leonard             German
  Reformed (Frederick County)
  Lischy          wit Benj Swoope, Jost Runckel


156    April 14, 1762          April 8, 1762          DD- 2,87
Zoll, Henrich              of Frederick County, German, a member
  Lutheran, in our Church on the Ambrosis Creek
  Beck          wit Conrad Hackenshmid, George Schmid, Andreas Rau


157    April 14, 1762          April 11- 1762          DD- 2,87
Doll, Conrad              German
Doll, Jacob               German
  Reformed (Frederick Town)
  Otterbein      wit Henrich Shober, Johannes Gomber


158    April 14, 1762          April 11, 1762          DD- 2,87
Baulus, Andreas            of Frederick County, German, a member
  Lutheran, in the Congregation in Canago
  Bager          wit Frid Gleiks, Jacob Schubb


159    April 14, 1762          April 4, 1762          DD- 2,87
Feit, Ulrich              German
Hoopman, Jacob             German
Zurbucher, Henrich           German
  Reformed (Fredericks County)
  Lischy        wit Benja Swoope, Jost Renukel


160    April 14, 1762          March 20, 1762          DD- 2,87
Brown, Jacob Frederick        German, a member
Littig, Philip            German, a member
Schwartz, William           German, a member
Williams, Johann Nicholaus Jr.  German, a member
Williams, Johann Nicholaus Sr.  German, a member
  Lutheran (Baltimore County)
  Kirchner      wit Morice Wersler, Daniel Beriah


161    (September 10,) 1762     April 14, 1762          DD- 2,89
Bower, Stephen
Cramlick, Jacob
Finger, Peter
Hartwake, George
Keener, Melchor

Metzler, Daniel
Rorer, John                    communion only
Whitmire, Michael
 St. Anne's, by the Rector of All Saints'
 Bacon          wit Charles Bryan, George Bager

162    (September 10,) 1762    April 14, 1762        DD- 2,89
Bager, Rev. George
Bishop, John
Miller, George
 St. Anne's, by the Rector of All Saints'
 Bacon          wit Charles Bryan, Melcher Kiner

163    (September 10,) 1762    April 14, 1762        DD- 2,89
Funk, Henry
Hefner, Michael
Zackarias, Mathias
 St. Anne's, by the Rector of All Saints'
 Bacon          wit Charles Bryan, Joachim Strover

164    (September 10,) 1762    April 14, 1762        DD- 2,89
Strever, Joachim
 St. Anne's, by the Rector of All Saints'
 Bacon          wit Charles Bryan, Michael Hoftner

165    (September 10,) 1762    April 11, 1762        DD- 2,89
Smith, Philip                  a member
Woolf, Paul                    a member
 Reformed, Frederick Town
 Otterbein      wit Thomas Schley, Johannes Gomber, Henrich Schober

166    (September 10,) 1762    April 14, 1762        DD- 2,89
Becker, Jonas
 St. Anne's
 Keene          wit Charles Bryan, John Fullford

167    (April 10,) 1762        April 11, 1762        DD- 2,93
Delaterre, Jacob               (of Anne Arundel County), German, a member
Geist, George                  (of Anne Arundel County), German, a member
Jeem, John                     a member, communion only
Pfister, Henrick               (of Anne Arundel County), German, a member
Sayler, Matthew                (of Anne Arundel County), German, a member
Smith, Jacob                   a member, communion only
Tick, Conrod                   (of Anne Arundel County), German, a member
 Reformed, Frederick Town
 Otterbein      wit Thomas Schley, Henrich Schober

168                          April 11, 1762            DD- 2,94
Wall, Henry                  communion only
Reformed, Congregation in the mountains
Otterbein      wit Thomas Schley, Henrich Shober


169    (April 10,) 1762      (March 7, 1762)           DD- 2,93
Marter, Valentine            of Frederick County, German, a member
Cananagan in York County
Bager          wit Frid Gelwicks, Conrad Kiefaber


170    (April 10,) 1762      April 19, 1762            DD- 2,93
Hochel, Justice              of Anne Arundel County, German
Power, Henry                 of Frederick County, German
Younger, Lewis               of Anne Arundel County, German
St. Anne's
Keene          wit Charles Bryan, Henry Bauer


171    (April 10,) 1762      April 20, 1762            DD- 2,93
Pope, John Grisman           of Frederick County, German
St. Anne's
Keene          wit Henry Bauer, Valtin Mader


172    September 15, 1762                              DD- 2,346
Abaugh, John                 of Frederick County, German
Moravian


173    September 15, 1762    September 5, 1762         DD- 2,346
Herbogh, Jacob               of Frederick County, German
Reformed, Frederick Town (Herbogh not a member, affirmed oath)
Otterbein      wit Thomas Schley, Johannes Gomber, Henrich Shober


174    September 15, 1762    July 31, 1762             DD- 2,346
Veillard, Peter              farmer at Manochasy, German
Moravian
Bohler         wit Lorentz Krieger, Caspar Schinrich, Lorentz Protzman


175    September 15, 1762    September 14, 1762        DD- 2,347
Fir, Joseph                  of Frederick County
Hamond, John                 of Frederick County
Mire, John                   of Frederick County
Shuet, Conrad                of Frederick County
St. Anne's
Keene


176    September 15, 1762    September 5, 1762         DD- 2,347
Engleman, Ludovicus          of Baltimore County
Fischer, Georgius            of Baltimore County

Fischer, Michael               of Baltimore County
Grohe, Christopher             of Baltimore County
Mengen, Georgius Phillippus    of Baltimore County
Sens, Christianus              of Baltimore County
Stein, Henricus                of Baltimore County
  Lutheran (Canawagda)
  Bager        wit Peter Faubib, Valentine Wentz

177    September 15, 1762      September 5, 1762      DD- 2,347
Damer, Christian               of Baltimore County, a member
Schlorpp, Peter                of Frederick County, a member
  Lutheran, Baltimore Town
  Kirchner     wit Johannes Allgeier, Adam Schort

178    September 15, 1762      September 5, 1762      DD- 2,347
Beckenbogh, Peter              of Frederick County, a member
Clementz, Valentine            of Frederick County, a member
Crepel, Peter                  of Frederick County, a member
Deener, John                   of Frederick County, a member
Hainz, John                    of Frederick County, a member
Hoover, Leonhard               of Frederick County, a member
Juda, Weinbert                 of Frederick County, a member
Kramar, Jacob                  of Frederick County, a member
Lingenfelther, Bernard         of Frederick County, a member
Shou, John                     of Frederick County, a member
  Reformed, Frederick Town
  Otterbein    wit Thomas Schley, Henrich Shober, Johannes Gomber

179    September 15, 1762      September 5, 1762      DD- 2,347
Gebhart, Mathias               of Baltimore County
  Lutheran, Baltimore Town
  Kirchner     wit Morice Wersler, Jacob Lamb

180    September 15, 1762      July 11, 1762         DD- 2,347
Faub, Peter                    of Baltimore County
Hank, Jacobus                  communion only
Tuchman, Stephan               of Baltimore County
Wentz, Valentine               of Baltimore County
  Lutheran (Canawagen)
  Bager        wit Christof Reinman, Pater ---an, Daniel Zapff

181    September 15, 1762      September 12, 1762    DD- 2, 347
Shreiber, Conrod               of Baltimore County
  Reformed
  Lischy       wit Daniel C--nor, Ulrich Huber

182    September 15, 1762      August 29, 1762       DD- 2,347

```
Bast, Valentine              of Frederick County
Bander, Peter                of Frederick County
Cooper, Daniel               of Frederick County
Ecklor, Jacob                of Baltimore County
Ecklor, Ulrick               of Baltimore County
Fischer, John                of Baltimore County
Fisser, Jacob                of Baltimore County
Gouches, Michael             of Frederick County
Groal, Peter                 of Frederick County
Kemp, Nicholas               of Frederick County
Loar, Herman                 communion only
Wohner, Peter                of Frederick County
 Reformed
Lischy          wit Ludwig Schreiber, --- Fehr


183     September 15, 1762      September 15, 1762      DD- 2,347
Chambert, Jacob              of Frederick County
Frank, Michael               of Frederick County
 Reformed, "Neapolis, Maryland"
Lischy          wit Conrad Schriber, --- Fehr, John Hammond


184     September 16, 1762      September 15, 1762      DD- 2,350
Judy, John                   of Frederick County, German
Klankerwick, William         of Frederick County, German
Schley, George               of Frederick County, German
 Reformed, "Neapolis, Maryland"
Lischy          wit A. Grunburt, Leonard Huber


185     September 16, 1762      September (  ,) 1762    DD- 2,350
Shaul, Sebastian             of Frederick County, German, a member
Weimar, Frederick            of Frederick County, German, a member
 Reformed, Cunngozee
Otterbein       wit David Jones Jr., Frederick Goerz


186     September 16, 1762      September 6, 1762       DD- 2,350
Bags, George                 of Frederick County, German
Harsh, Frederick             of Frederick County, German
 Lutheran Congregation at Fort Frederick
Shlotz          wit Johannes Mayr, Heinrich Heintzman


187     September 18, 1762      September 12, 1762      DD- 2,351
Schrink, Peter               German, a member
 Reformed
Otterbein       wit Heinrich Griting, Abraham ---


188     September 21, 1762      September 5, 1762       DD- 2,351
Bucher, Peter                German, a member
```

Deame, John                    German, a member
Everhott, Christopher          German, a member
Fitler, Valentine              German, a member
Raybuck, John                  German, a member
Smith, Jacob                   German, a member
Young, Conrad                  German, a member
  Schlotz        wit (Dein Tabel), Conrad Coon


189    September 21, 1762       August 15, 1762          DD- 2,351
Krype, Jacob                   German
Mire, Jacob                    German
  (Annapitist at Canogochiquon)
  N. Martin      wit Michael Miller, Jacob Miller


190    September 23, 1762       August 8, 1762           DD- 2,352
Miller, Lodwig                 of Frederick County, German, a member
Roderick, Lodwig               of Frederick County, German, a member
  Baptist Congregation in Frederick County
  Roland         wit Daniel Leatherman, Andoni Hartman


191    September 24, 1762       September 5, 1762         DD- 2,352
Darr, George                   of Frederick County, German
Hildebrand, John               of Frederick County, German
Humbert, William               of Frederick County, German
  Reformed, Frederick Town
  Otterbein      wit Thomas Schley, Christian Kayser


192    September 24, 1762       September 5, 1762         DD- 2,352
Gyser, Christopher             of Frederick County, German, a member
Hargate, Peter                 of Frederick County, German, a member
  Reformed, Frederick Town
  Otterbein      wit Thomas Schley, William Hunyroot


193    September 24, 1762       September 5, 1762         DD- 2,352
Putman, Andrew                 of Frederick County, German, a member
  Reformed, Frederick Town
  Otterbein      wit Thomas Schley, Peter Hergud


194    September 24, 1762       October 4, 1761          DD- 2,353
Richards, James                of Baltimore County, gentleman
  St. Thomas's


195    September 28, 1762       September 5, 1762         DD- 2,354
Coplenz, Peter                 of Frederick County, German, a member
Holzman, Frederick             of Frederick County, German, a member
Leahman, Jacob                 of Frederick County, German, a member

Witterick, Martin          of Frederick County, German, a member
Reformed, Frederick Town
Otterbein       wit Thomas Schley, Henrich Gomber, Lennard Keller

196    September 28, 1762        June 20, 1762          DD- 2,354
Stooker, Michael              of Frederick County, German
Lutheran, Frederick Town
Harwich        wit Conrad Grosh, Balthasar Bonz

197    September 29, 1762        September 29, 1762     DD- 2,355
Couperight, George Peter       of Frederick County, German
Fast, Nicholas                 of Frederick County, German
Pickenpagh, Leonard            of Frederick County, German
Rop, Michael                   of Frederick County, German
Smith, David                   of Frederick County, German
St. Anne's
Keene          wit Jacob ---

198    September 29, 1762        September 12, 1762     DD- 2,355
King, Abraham                  of Frederick County, German
Reformed, Congregation at Kanigochiquon
Otterbein      wit Johannes Gomber, Henrich Shober, Abraham Lingenfelter

199    September 29, 1762        August 29, 1762       DD- 2,355
Foub, Nicholas                 of Frederick County, German
Lutheran, Congregation at Kitocting
Schlets        wit Andrew Grimm, Johannes Schmid--, Abraham Lingenfelder

200    September 30, 1762        September 12, 1762     DD- 2,355
Asby, Rudolph                  of Frederick County, German, a member
Snavely, Henry                 of Frederick County, German, a member
Reformed, Congregation at Cangochique
Otterbein      wit Jacob Zoller, David Heger

201    April 13, 1762           April 9, 1763          DD- 3,125
Stoler, John                 German
Stouber, John William        German
St. Paul's
Chase          wit Henry Zwinglius, Andrew Finger, Friedrich Meyer

202    April 13, 1763           April 1, 1763          DD- 3,125
Calman, John Rudy            German
Calman, Mathias              German
St. Paul's
Chase          wit Conrad Schmidt, Friedrich Weinbert Tschudi

203    April 13, 1763           April 1, 1763          DD- 3,125

Pentz, Adam                German
Clentz, Henry              German
 Reformed (York Town)
 Wirts          wit Martin Tanner, Heinrich ---, Philip Foss


204    April 13, 1763         April 3, 1763          DD- 3,125
Humer, Jacob               German, a member
Smith, Philip              German, a member
 Reformed, Frederick Town
 Otterbein     wit Thomas Schley, Valentine Adams, Johannes Gomber


205    April 13, 1763         April 3, 1763          DD- 3,125
Adams, Valentine           German, a member
 Reformed, Frederick Town
 Otterbein     wit Johannes Gomber, Loudwig Weltner, Stephan Remesperger
               wit Abraham Lingenfelter


206    April 13, 1763         March 27, 1763         DD- 3,125
Loewe, George Adam         German
Volk, Ulrich               German
 (Baltimore Town)
 Kirchner      wit Samuel --- Tschnedi, Morice Wersler


207    April 13, 1763         April 3, 1763          DD- 3,125
Wigil, Sebastian           German, a member
 Reformed, Frederick County
 Otterbein     wit Ludy ---, Abraham Lingenfeld, Rapham Rumensperger


208    April 13, 1763         April 1, 1763          DD- 3,125
Foss, Philip               German
Hirsh, Conrad              German
Smatt, Matthias            German
Stoltz, Niclaus            German
 Reformed (York Town)
 Wirt          wit Martin Deaner, Henrich Klentz


209    April 13, 1763         April 3, 1763          DD- 3,125
Risner, Tobias             German, a member
 Reformed, Frederick County
 Otterbein     wit Ludwid Ebentiner, Abraham Lingenfelder
               wit Rapham Remesperger


210    April 13, 1763         April 3, 1763          DD- 3,125
Swarts, Andrew             German, a member
 Reformed, Frederick Town
 Otterbein     wit Rapham Rimenspirger, (Ludidy Swinner)
               wit Abraham Lingenfelder

211     April 13, 1763          April 4, 1763          DD- 3,125
Frosh, George                    German
Snider, Frederick                German
Snider, Martin                   German
 Reformed (York County)
 Lischy          wit Ben Swoope, Joss Runckel


212     April 13, 1763          April 3, 1763          DD- 3,125
Blumenschein, John               of Frederick County, German, a member
Schmid, Michael                  of Frederick County, German, a member
Scholl, Michael                  of Frederick County, German, a member
Schumaker, George                of Frederick County, German, a member
 Lutheran, Church on Little Pfeif Creek
 Beck          wit (Jacob Bernauer), Johannes ---


213     April 13, 1763          April 13, 1763          DD- 3,125
Andrews, William                 of Frederick County, German
Basteon, Andrew                  of Frederick County, German
Coblens, Philip                  of Frederick County, German
Erb, Peter                       of Frederick County, German
Hyle, John                       of Frederick County, German
Onstend, George                  of Frederick County, German
Opercock, Jacob                  of Baltimore County, German
Tillingen, George                of Frederick County, German
Woolf, John                      of Frederick County, German
 St. Anne's
 Keene          wit Samuel Blumnenschein, Gerg Schumacher


214     April 13, 1763          March 31, 1763          DD- 3,125
Laurer, Gotfrid                  of Frederick County, German, a member
 Lutheran, Little Pfeif Creek
 Bech          wit Jerg Wirter, (Ludwig Ebentimer), (Jacob Bernauer)
                wit (Johannes Grider)


215     April 15, 1763          April 15, 1763          DD- 3,129
Engul, Peter                     of Frederick County, German
Tallenbok, Samuel                of Frederick County, German
 St. Anne's
 Keene          wit Jacob Bowlis, Peter Engul


216     April 15, 1763          April 14, 1763          DD- 3,129
Wherton Backer, Bernard          of Frederick County, German
Powlis, Jacob                    of Frederick County, German
 St. Anne's
 Keene          wit Jacob Baulus, Berhard Wernalkebucher


217     April 15, 1763          April 15, 1763          DD- 3,129

Craner, Michael          German
  Chase          wit Jacob Tinz, John Coxe

218    April 21, 1763          April 11, 1763          DD- 3,130
Wirt, Casper          German, a member
Wirt, Jacob          German, a member
Reformed, Frederick Town
Otterbein      wit Thomas Schley, Henrich Schober

219    April 27, 1763          April 3, 1763          DD- 3,130
Clementz, Leonard          of Frederick County, German, a member
Frederick Town
Otterbein      wit Thomas Schley, Johannes Gomber, Henrich Shober

220    April 27, 1763          within three months      DD- 3,130
Judy, Philip          of Fred. Cnty. and Cotocton Hundred, German
Lutheran
Slitz          wit Conrath Korn, Peter ---

221    September 14, 1763          DD- 4,133
Albert, John Jacob          German
Apple, Peter          German
Gratener, Henry          German
Hagar, John          German
Kuntz, Peter          German
Poussum, Lawrance          German
Shwegheler, George          German
St. Anne's
Dowie          wit Robert Chalmers, Philip Williams

222    September 14, 1763      September 11, 1763      DD- 4,133
Zapff, Daniel          German
Reformed (York County)
Lischy          wit George Lingenfelder, Johannes Keller

223    September 14, 1763      September 11, 1763      DD- 4,133
Goehmung, Andreas          German
Straubell, Zachariah          German
Lutheran (Baltimore County)
Kirchner          wit Moritz Wersler, Johans Hamill

224    September 14, 1763      September 12, 1763      DD- 4,133
Beck, Joseph          German
Hauser, Casper          German
Zimmerman, George          German
(Baltimore County)
Kirchner      wit Johannes Allgeyer, Andreas Geppescheimer, Edward Smith

225    September 14, 1763        September 12, 1763        DD- 4,133
Clows, William                  German
Teal, Christian                 German
  St. Paul's
  Chase          wit Friedrich Meyer, Teowald Berger

226    September 14, 1763        September 12, 1763        DD- 4,133
Schmidt, Edward
  Lutheran (Baltimore County)
  Kirchner        wit Johannes Allgeyer, George Zimmerman
                  wit Andreas Geppenheimer

227    September 14, 1763        September 11, 1763        DD- 4,133
Shield, Charles                 German
Timberman, Mathias              German
  St. Paul's
  Chase          wit Jonas Odenback, Marti Tschudi

228    September 14, 1763        September 11, 1763        DD- 4,133
Chudy, Martin                   German
  St. Paul's
  Chase          wit Jonas Odenbach, Carl Shiel

229    September 14, 1763        September 3, 1763         DD- 4,133
Hush, Valentine                 German
  St. Paul's
  Chase          wit William Piper, Jos Odenback

230    September 14, 1763        September 3, 1763         DD- 4,133
Piper, William                  German
  St. Paul's
  Chase          wit Vallentin Hueh, Jos Shrep

231    September 14, 1763        September 11, 1763        DD- 4,133
Odenbaugh, Jonas                German
  St. Paul's
  Chase          wit Carl Shiel, Martin Tchudi

232    September 14, 1763        September 11, 1763        DD- 4,133
Bott, Wendel                    of Fred. Cnty., German, mbr. at Mittel Creek
Danner, Michael                 of Fred. Cnty., German, mbr. at Mittel Creek
Zigler, George                  of Fred. Cnty., German, mbr. at Mittel Creek
  Lutheran Church in Anthonis Thawn
  Beck            wit Jno Wever, Jacob Crook, Saml Emrich Bott

233    September 14, 1763        July 31, 1763            DD- 4,133
Schaefer, Christian             German

Lutheran (Baltimore County)
Kirchner        wit Anthony Nole, Michal Bart, Michael Dirk, Jacob Utz

234    September 14, 1763       August 7, 1763         DD- 4,133
Haan, George                    of Frederick County, German, a member
Lutheran, Church on Silver Ront
Beck            wit Johannes Hahn, Jacob Brecker

235    September 14, 1763       August 7, 1763         DD- 4,133
Doorn, Georg Michael            of Fred. Cnty., German, mbr. at Silber Runte
Hahn, John                      of Fred. Cnty., German, mbr. at Silber Runte
Herman, George                  of Fred. Cnty., German, mbr. at Silber Runte
Lutheran
Beck           wit John Lewis, Daniel Stern, Jacob Bencker, Leinhard Zug

236    September 14, 1763       September 8, 1763      DD- 4,133
England, Abraham                German
St. Paul's
Chase          wit Henry Shutter, Saml Dun

237    September 14, 1763       April 4, 1763          DD- 4,133
Bonner, Philip                  German
Reformed
Lischy         wit Jost Runckel, Bena Swoope

238    September 14, 1763       August 7, 1763         DD- 4,133
Steiner, George                 of Frederick County, German, a member
Lutheran, Silber Round
Beck           wit Georg Michael ---, Johannes Hahn

239    September 15, 1763       September 14, 1763     DD- 4,136
Coppersmith, John               German
Reyley, Burghart                German
Reyley, John                    German
Seiler, Jacob                   German
St. Anne's
Dowie          wit Timothy Carinton, Philip Williams

240    September 21, 1763       September 20, 1763     DD- 4,137
Michael, Nicholas               of Frederick County, German
Wooph, Martin                   of Frederick County, German
St. Anne's
Dowie          wit Valentine Shraner, Philip Williams

241    September 21, 1763       last 5 days of July    DD- 4,137
Bigler, Michael                 of Frederick County, German, a member
Schepfell, Michael              of Frederick County, German, a member

Baptist Congregation of Frederick County
Leatherman     wit Daniel Arnold, Andon Hartman

242    September 28, 1763        September 28, 1763        DD- 4,137
Farmer, Christian            of Frederick County, German
Michael, Christopher         of Frederick County, German
Weild, George                of Frederick County, German
Woolfin, Christiph           of Frederick County, German
Yeildinbrand, Adam           of Frederick County, German
  St. Anne's
  Dowie          wit Philip Williams, Thomas Creekmaster

243    April 11, 1764           April (12,) 1764         DD- 5,282
Hickleman, Michael           German
Michael, Andrew              German
Rigor, John                  German
Rodenbeler, Philip           German
  St. Anne's
  Dowie          wit Philip Williams, Nathaniel Waters

244    April 11, 1764           March 7, 1764            DD- 5,282
Benkele, Peter               farmer at Monokosy, German
  Moravian
  Beahler        wit Jacob Bockman, Andres Rurtscher, Jacob Wiber

245    April 11, 1764           April 6, 1764            DD- 5,282
Boyerle, Conrod              German, a member
Boyerle, Ludy                a member, communion only
Einsler, Henry               German, a member
Frosch, Sebastian            German, a member
  Lutheran, York Town
  Hornell        wit Adam Schock, Johan Peter Schnepf

246    April 11, 1764           March 25, 1764           DD- 5,282
Huebner, Adam                of Frederick County, member, communion only
Huebner, Michael             of Frederick County, German, a member
Kiefer, Christian            of Frederick County, German, a member
Ries, Andreas                of Frederick County, German, a member
Ries, Thomas                 of Frederick County, German, a member
Winters, Eva Maria           of Fred. Cnty., German, widow of George, mbr
  Lutheran, Church on the Peiff Creek
  Beck           wit Fritterig Hendman, John Grider, Jacob Bernauer

247    April 11, 1764           April 4, 1764            DD- 5,282
Frey, George                 German
  Reformed (Catores Township, York County)
  Lischy         wit Peter Runk, Peter Finger, Friedrich Roemer

248    April 11, 1764          April 4, 1764              DD- 5,282
Hauk, Jacob                     German, a member
Nunemaker, Jacob                German, a member
 Lutheran, Jacob's Church, Cadores Township
 Hornell      wit Daniel Cramer ---, Stuffal Rodamal, Peter Finger

249    April 11, 1764          April (16,) 1764           DD- 5,282
Farmer, Peter                   German
Main, George                    German
Toffeller, George               German
 St. Anne's
 Dowie        wit Philip Williams, Phillip Rodenbuhler

250    April 11, 1764          April (18,) 1764           DD- 5,282
Berger, Philip                  German
Everlie, John                   German
Heartman, Joseph                German
Sinn, Jacob                     German
 St. Anne's
 Dowie        wit Philip Williams, Phillib Rodenbuhler

251    May 2, 1764             April 22, 1764             DD- 5,282
Vallette, Mr. Elie              German
 St. Anne's
 Dowie        wit Thos Lyttleton, Philip Williams

252    September 12, 1764      September 12, 1764         DD- 6,281
Bruter, Jacob                   German
Klein, Frederick                German
Rod, Jacob                      German
Tanner, Michael                 German
 St. Anne's
 Love         wit Philip Williams, Stephen Matthis

253    September 12, 1764      September 4, 1764          DD- 6,281
Bell, Anthonius                 of Frederick County, German
Cammerer, Ludwig                German, communion only
Giesert, Frederick              of Frederick County, German
Huber, Adam                     of Frederick County, German
Kohler, George                  of Frederick County, German
Mong, Nicklas                   of Frederick County, German
Ritter, Jacob                   of Frederick County, German
Stephan, Andreas                of Frederick County, German
Vogler, John Frederick          of Frederick County, German
 Lutheran, Frederick County
 Shwordfeger   wit Conrad Hogmire, Ludetig Funk, Dewald Scheffer

254     September 12, 1764          September 9, 1764          DD- 6,281
Stoler, Werther                     German, a member
 Frederick Town
 Otterbein      wit Georg Hoffman, Georg Lingenfelter

255     September 12, 1764          September 4, 1764          DD- 6,281
Welchenbach, Reinhard               of Frederick County, German, a member
 Lutheran, Frederick County
 Shwordfeger    wit Mathias Spangler, Matthias Rud

256     September 12, 1764          August 26, 1764           DD- 6,281
Willhelm, Nicolaus                  of Frederick County, German, a member
 Lutheran, in our Church on Mittel Creek
 Beck           wit Jacob Bernauer, Georg Born

257     September 13, 1764          April 22, 1764            DD- 6,283
Kenckele, Frederick                 resident of Frederick Town, German
Wetzel, Martin                      resident of Frederick Town, German
 Lutheran, Frederick Town
 Shwordfeger    wit Friedrich Dannwolf, Michael Roemer

258     September 17, 1764          September 9, 1764          DD- 6,284
Han, Jacob                          German, a member
Knobel, Philip                      German, a member
 Reformed, Frederick Town
 Otterbein      wit Stephan Ransburger, Georg Hoffman, Henrich Schober
                wit Georg Lingenfelter

259     September 17, 1764          September 9, 1764          DD- 6,284
Bickenbach, John Adam               German, a member
Bickinbachin, Anna Maria            German, a member
Hoffman, Georg                      German, a member
Waldner, Lutwick                    German, a member
 Reformed, Frederick Town
 Otterbein      wit Stephen Ransburger, Georg Lingenfelter

260     September 18, 1764          September 2, 1764          DD- 6,285
Berkman, Peter                      German, a member
 Reformed, member in my Congregation at Andiedem Creek
 Otterbein      wit Thomas Schley, Valentine Stocke

261     September 18, 1764          September 17, 1764         DD- 6,285
Byer, Hubertus                      German
Potts, Ludwick                      German
Sonfrank, Jacob                     German
 St. Anne's
 Love           wit Philip Williams, Valentine Krueger

262    September 21, 1764        August 14, 1764        DD- 6,285
Grabeel, Joseph                 German, communion only
Teasher, Peter                  German
  Frederick County
  Gottrecht      wit George Martin, Fillip Fink


263    September 21, 1764        September 7, 1764       DD- 6,285
Davis, Johannes                 German, member at Conceges
Eydenuer, Johannes              German, member at Conceges
Flender, Johannes               German, member at Conceges
Hagar, David                    German, member at Conceges
Reber, Christoffel              German, member at Conceges
Schebely, Leonard               German, member at Conceges
Scheffer, George                German, member at Conceges
Senably, Henry                  German, member at Conceges
Stall, Henrick                  German, member at Conceges
Zimmerman, Jost                 German, member at Conceges
  Reformed, Frederick Town
  Otterbein      wit Stephen Rensperger, Georg Lingenfelter


264    September 21, 1764        September 4, 1764       DD- 6,285
Kamerer, Ludwig                 of Frederick County, German, a member
  Lutheran, Frederick Town
  Shwordfeger    wit Conrad Hogmire, Ludetig Funk, Dewald Scheffer


265    September 21, 1764        September 20, 1764      DD- 6,285
Weshenback, Henry               German
  St. Anne's
  Love          wit Philip Williams, Christian Orndorff


266    September 29, 1764        September 23, 1764      DD- 6,286
Heffner, John                   of Frederick County, German
Letter, John                    of Frederick County, German
  Lutheran, Frederick County
  Shwordfeger    wit Conrad Grosh, Michael Romer


267    September 29, 1764        September 2, 1764       DD- 6,286
Kuntz, William                  German
  St. Anne's
  Love          wit Philip Williams, Bartel Schumaker


268    September 29, 1764        September 9, 1764       DD- 6,286
Hufferner, Melechior            German, a member
Jacob, Franciscus               German, a member
Schumaker, Bartholomew          German, a member
  Reformed, Frederick Town

Otterbein     wit Georg Lingenfelter, Georg Huffman

269    April 10, 1765              April 9, 1765          DD- 7,280
Arthur, Michael                of Baltimore County, German
St. Paul's
Chase        wit Caspar Mayer, Georg Maten

270    July 17, 1765            July 15, 1765          DD- 7,280
Thomas, Frederick          German
Lutheran, Baltimore County
Kirchner      wit Johannes Schrien, John Heul

271    July 17, 1765            July 17, 1765          DD- 7,280
Fleck, George              German
Foy, Michael               German
Jockem, Andrew             German
Mueller, Michael           German
Panz, Adam                 German
Baltimore County
Kirchner      wit Jacob Dietrich, Adam Brant

272    July 17, 1765           (July 9, 1765)         DD- 7,280
Brand, Adam                of Baltimore County, German
Lutheran, Baltimore County
Shwordfeger   wit Jacob Dietrich, Friedrich Thomas

273    July 17, 1765            April 21, 1765         DD- 7,280
Walder, Jacob              resident of Frederick Town, German
Lutheran, Frederick Town
Shwordfeger   wit Conrad Grosh, Michael Koerner

274    July 17, 1765            July 13, 1765          DD- 7,280
Kirchner, Jasper           German
St. Paul's
Chase         wit Morice Werslor, Chls Fred Weisenthal

275    July 17, 1765            May 26, 1765           DD- 7,280
Steiner, Jacob             German, a member
Reformed, Frederick Town
Otterbein     wit Thomas Schley, Phillip Bier

276    July 17, 1765            July 15, 1765          DD- 7,280
Bier, Philip               German, a member
Reformed, Frederick Town
Otterbein     wit Johannes Gomber, John Weaver, Thomas Schley

277    July 17, 1765            July 2, 1765           DD- 7,280

Rohr, Rudolph               German, a member
  Reformed, Frederick Town
  Otterbein      wit Stephen Remsberger, Georg Lingenfelter, Georg Hoffman

278    July 17, 1765             April 21, 1765           DD- 7,280
Mayor, John Jeremiah           resident of Frederick Town, German
  Lutheran, Frederick Town
  Shwordfeger    wit Jacob Friedrich Dannwolf, Carl Schell

279    July 19, 1765             (June 26, 1765)          DD- 7,282
Miller, John                   of Frederick County, German
  Lutheran, Frederick County
  Shwordfeger    wit Nichelous Jacob, Andreas Buttman

280    July 19, 1765             June 17, 1765            DD- 7,1765
Burkitt, Michael               of Frederick County, German
  Lutheran, Frederick County
  Shwordfeger    wit Gottfried Lederman

281    September 3, 1765         September 3, 1765         DD- 7,283
Gardner, Christian             German
Keiffer, George                German
Krim, Alexander                German
Stall, Jacob                   German
Weaver, Christian              German
Weible, John                   German
Yoel, Henry                    German
  St. Anne's
  Love           wit James Chalmers, Philip Williams

282    September 3, 1765         August 29, 1765          DD- 7,283
Hysing, Jacob                  of Frederick County, German
  Lutheran, Frederick Town
  Shwordfeger

283    September 3, 1765         September 1, 1765         DD- 7,283
Hershman, Mathias              of Frederick County, German
  Lutheran, Frederick Town
  Shwordfeger    wit Conrad Grosh, Carl Schell

284    September 3, 1765         August 29, 1765          DD- 7,283
Croois, Christopher            resident of Sharpsburgh, German
Keifer, Frederick              resident of Sharpsburgh, German
Pfiffer, Jacob                 resident of Sharpsburgh, German
Saum, Nicholas                 resident of Sharpsburgh, German
Wiss, Detrick                  resident of Sharpsburgh, German
  Lutheran, Frederick County

Shwordfeger    wit Abraham Lingenfelter, Jacob ---

285    September 4, 1765        May 26, 1765            DD- 7,284
Lingenfelter, Valentine      of Frederick County, German, a member
Reformed, Frederick Town
Otterbein     wit Georg Hoffman, George Lingenfelter, Johannes Brunner

286    September 4, 1765        September 4, 1765      DD- 7,284
Bucher, Philip               of Frederick County, German
Kettleman, Christopher       of Frederick County, German
Snably, Conrod               of Frederick County, German
St. Anne's
Love          wit Jacob Stall, Philip Williams

287    September 4, 1765        August 29, 1765        DD- 7,284
Krazinger, George            resident of Sharpsburgh, German
Lutheran, Frederick County
Shwordfeger    wit Detrig Weiss, Valentine Lingenfelter

288    September 6, 1765        September 6, 1765      DD- 7,285
Burgunt, Simon               of Frederick County, German
Marts, Bastian               of Frederick County, German
Usselman, Valentine          of Frederick County, German
St. Anne's
Love          wit Hugh Maguire, Philip Williams

289    September 6, 1765        August 29, 1765        DD- 7,285
Blanck, Frederick            of Frederick County, German
Lutheran, Frederick County
Shwordfeger    wit Valti ---, Simon Burduck

290    September 11, 1765       September 1, 1765      DD- 9,2
Adam, John                   of Frederick County, German
member of the Society of Baptists
G. Martin     wit Johanes Horn, Nicklaus Fink

291    September 11, 1765       September 2, 1765      DD- 9,2
Ebersoll, Christian          of Frederick County, German
Graebal, Joseph              of Frederick County, German
G. Martin     wit Johannes Fink, John Horn

292    September 11, 1765       September 10, 1765     DD- 9,2
Albaugh, William
Andre, Peter
Angene, Devold
Ash, Henry
Becker, William

Berk, Handel
Boltzel, Henry
Boltzel, Jacob
Boltzel, Peter
Bower, Christian
Clindman, Til
Ester, Adam
Grindler, Philip
Grouse, William
Holts, Jacob
Hone, Gasper
Hopper, Cornelius
Hover, Vandal
Hysler, Nicholas
Karsner, George
Lamberd, George
Lons, George
Marts, George
Rice, Gasper
Rouch, John
Sheffer, Nicholas
Sly, Jacob
Tegarden, William
 St. Anne's
 Love           wit Phillip ---, Philip Williams


293    September 11, 1765        September 1, 1765        DD- 9,2
Fortine, Catherine            resident of Frederick Town, German
Hartman, Margaret             resident of Frederick Town, German
 Lutheran
 Shwordfeger    wit Conrad Grosh, Carl Schell


294    September 11, 1765        September 1, 1765        DD- 9,2
Kolb, Michael                 resident of Frederick Town, German
 Lutheran, Frederick Town
 Shwordfeger    wit Conrad Grosh, Carl Schell


295    September 11, 1765        August 17, 1765         DD- 9,2
Hooghe, William
Huber, Ulrich                 communion only
Knaufe, Henrick
Miller, Christian
Renner, Adam
Slick, John
 Reformed, Danys Town
 Lischy         wit Fehillib Brunner, Johannes Schroyer

296     September 11, 1765     September 11, 1765     DD- 9,3
Boon, Nichole
Braker, John
Cost, Felty
Cost, George
Flood, Michael
Goval, Frederick
Haman, Philip
Harman, Marricks
Herman, Jacob
Hickerel, Herman
Hoffman, Adam
Hoffman, Henry
Hoffman, Peter
Keller, Rudulph
Kuntz, Henry
Lingenfelder, George
Low, Herman
Motterel, George
Occulberry, Abraham
Pecker, Peter
Powell, Barnard
Powell, Philip
Roct, Christian
Rosenplater, John Herman
Rungle, Jacob
Shingle, Lawrance
Steekle, Simon
Tickel, Michael
Tickensheets, William
Tups, Oswal
Wicknar, John
Wilk, George
 St. Anne's
 Love          wit Fbl Grimwold, Philip Williams


297     September 11, 1765     10 post Trinitas     DD- 9,3
Ritter, Ludovicus
 Lutheran (Baltimore County)
 Kirchner       wit Jacob Walthen, Carl Schmid


298     September 11, 1765     August 9, 1765     DD- 9,3
Freck, Philip           of Frederick County, German
Hartner, John           of Frederick County, German
Hupp, Augustus          of Frederick County, German
Ott, Michael            of Frederick County, German
Russ, Michael           of Frederick County, German

Shwartz, Frederick          of Frederick County, German, communion only
Toftman, Martin             of Frederick County, German
  Lutheran, Frederick County
  Shwordfeger   wit Jacob Mathis, Andreas Raw

299    September 11, 1765        August 28, 1765        DD- 9,3
Bell, Peter                 of Frederick County, German, communion only
Huber, Adam                 of Frederick County, German
Huber, Peter                of Frederick County, German
Stephan, Leonard            of Frederick County, German
  Lutheran, Frederick County
  Shwordfeger   wit Caspar Wagoner, Berhard Lickhard

300    September 11, 1765        August 28, 1765        DD- 9,3
Roof, Anthony               of Frederick County, German
Shees, Peter                of Frederick County, German
Snider, John                of Frederick County, German
Wagoner, Casper             of Frederick County, German
  Lutheran, Frederick County
  Shwordfeger   wit Lonhard Stephan, Bernhard Lickhard

301    September 11, 1765        August 28, 1765        DD- 9,3
Somer, Ludwick              of Frederick County, German
  Lutheran
  Shwordfeger   wit Friedrich ---, Walter ---

302    September 11, 1765        August 21, 1765        DD- 9,3
Hummel, John                resident of Frederick Town, German
  Lutheran, Frederick Town
  Shwordfeger   wit Carl Schell, Conrad Grosh, Michael Roemer

303    September 11, 1765        September 1, 1765       DD- 9,3
Bander, Leonard             of Frederick County, German
Roos, Christian             of Frederick County, German
Row, Erhard                 of Frederick County, German
  Lutheran
  Shwordfeger   wit Jacob Mathis, Andreas Raw

304    September 11, 1765        September 1, 1765       DD- 9,3
Beem, Adam                  of Frederick County, German
Boulus, Nicholas            of Frederick County, German
Domer, Michael              of Frederick County, German
Farber, Philip              of Frederick County, German
Louffer, Gotlip             of Frederick County, German
Louffer, Michael            of Frederick County, German
Reehl, Frederick            of Frederick County, German
Roller, John                of Frederick County, German

Shaffer, Philip Jacob      of Frederick County, German
Shleetzer, Jacob           of Frederick County, German
Shulz, Daniel              of Frederick County, German
Souder, Felix              of Frederick County, German
Stone, John                of Frederick County, German
Wisshaar, George           of Frederick County, German
 Lutheran
 Shwordfeger   wit Conrad Grosh, Carl Schell

305    September 11, 1765      June 23, 1765          DD- 9,3
Kisle, Lenard              of Hydleburg Township, York County
Klabsattle, Michael        of Mt. Pleasant Township, York County
Shoop, Jacob               of Mt. Pleasant Township, York County
Salomonsmiller, Ludwick    of Manheim Township, York County
 Lutheran, Little Conawaga
 Bager          wit Frid Gelwick, Yost Waggoner

306    September 11, 1765      August 28, 1765        DD- 9,3
Leckhard, Barnhard         of Frederick County, German
Raymel, Philip             of Frederick County, German
Reeber, William            of Frederick County, German
 Lutheran, Frederick County
 Shwordfeger    wit Caspar Wagner, Lenhard Stephan

307    September 11, 1765      September 1, 1765      DD- 9,3
Bott, Emrich               of Frederick County, German, communion only
Brown, Henry               of Pint-Run Hundred, Fred. Cnty., German
Hammer, Francis            of Frederick County, German
Krise, Stephen             resident of Germany Twp., York Cnty., German
Long, Adam                 of Frederick County, German
Lows, Christopher          of Frederick County, German
Mahring, Woolfgang         of Frederick County, German
Marklin, John              of Frederick County, German
Marklin, Nicholas          of Frederick County, German
Martin, George             resident of Germany Twp., York Cnty., German
Smith, Philip              of Frederick County, German
Zyer, Matthias             of Frederick County, German
 Lutheran
 Wildbahne     wit Georg Ziegler, Wendel Bott

308    September 11, 1765      August 28, 1765        DD -9,3
Leiser, Mathias            of Frederick County, German
                           also referred to Henry Leiser
Thom, Henrick              of Frederick County, German
 Lutheran
 Shwordfeger   wit Adam Huber, Caspar Wagner

309     September 11, 1765        August 18, 1765          DD- 9,3
Hardlis, George               a member
Miller, John                  a member
Nicodemus, Frederick          a member
Seitz, Wendle                 a member
 Reformed, Congregation in Conogochick
 Otterbein     wit Henry Shnebely, Davit Heger


310     September 11, 1765        May 26, 1765             DD- 9,3
Walter, Henrick               a member
 Reformed, Frederick Town
 Otterbein     wit Georg Lingenfelter, Georg Hoffman, Valentin Adam


311     September 11, 1765        August 28, 1765          DD- 9,3
Bouman, Simon                 of Frederick County, German
 Lutheran
 Shwordfeger    wit Friedrich Dannwolf, Martin Jacob


312     September 11, 1765        August 18, 1765          DD- 9,3
Adam, Johannes                a member
Shnebely, Conrad              a member, communion only
Zoller, Jacob                 a member
 Reformed
 Otterbein        wit Henry Shnebely, --- Heger


313     September 11, 1765        August 28, 1765          DD- 9,3
Bishop, Jacob                 of Frederick County, German, communion only
Helsenstine, Nicholas         of Frederick County, German, communion only
Jacob, Martin                 of Frederick County, German
Keeler, George                of Frederick County, German
 Lutheran
 Shwordfeger    wit Antoni Rupt, Peter (Shutz)


314     September 11, 1765        August 28, 1765          DD- 9,3
Gebhart, Andrew               of Frederick County, German, communion only
Kessinger, Mathias            of Frederick County, German
Shwenk, Casper                of Frederick County, German, communion only
Wacker, Jacob                 of Frederick County, German, communion only
 Lutheran, Frederick County
 Shwordfeger    wit Johan ---, Friederich (Hanz)


315     September 12, 1765        July 13, 1765            DD- 9,16
Weisenthall, Charles          of Baltimore County, German
                              Dr. Charles Frederic Weisenthall
 St. Paul's
 Chase        wit Morice Wersler, Joh. Casp. Kirchner

316     September 12, 1765          August 18, 1765          DD- 9,17
Graft, George                      of Frederick County, German, a member
member of the people called Unitas Fratrum (Baptist)
Laetherman     wit Daniel Arnold, Johannes Grossnickel

317     September 13, 1765          August 28, 1765          DD- 9,17
Bell, Peter                        of Frederick County, German
Keeler, George                     of Frederick County, German
Wacker, Jacob                      of Frederick County, German
Lutheran
Shwordfeger   wit Ludvig Funk, Johan Stefhan Bell

318     September 16, 1765          September 14, 1765          DD- 9,18
Bender, George                     German
Little, Gasper                     German
Littler, Henry                     German
Rorback, Jacob                     German
Shilley, Jacob                     German
St. Anne's
Love          wit George Mitchell, Philip Williams

319     September 18, 1765          August 17, 1765          DD- 9,19
Huber, Ulrich                      German
Reformed (Danis Town)
Lischy        wit Fehlbib Brunner, Hanes Schroeyer

320     September 18, 1765          September 18, 1765          DD- 9,19
Fry, Henry                         German
Hersman, Henry                     German
St. Anne's
Love          wit Ulrich Huber, Philip Williams

321     September 20, 1765          September 20, 1765          DD- 9,19
Hoyl, Andrew                       German
Lebelly, Michael                   German
Ruet, George                       German
Ruet, Jacob                        German
St. Anne's
Love          wit Hugh Maguire, Philip Williams

322     September 24, 1765          September 24, 1765          DD- 9,20
Brown, Stofold                     German
Green, Gerard                      German
Gysinger, John                     German
Hill, Peter                        German
St. Anne's
Love          wit Philip Williams, Wiliam Humpert

323     September 24, 1765        September 24, 1765      DD- 9,20
Crist, Jacob                     German
Crist, Michael                   German
Crist, Philip                    German
Frushower, Jacob                 German
Troutman, Peter                  German
  St. Anne's
  Love            wit James Davison, Philip Williams


324     September 26, 1765        September 26, 1765      DD- 9,43
Craw, Conrad                     German
Delauder, Lawrance               German
Keller, Abraham                  German
Keller, John                     German
Short, John                      German
Rinamon, Christopher             German
  St. Anne's
  Love            Philip Williams


325     September 26, 1765        June 23, 1765          DD- 9,43
Hower, Michael                   German
Kramer, Helfry                   German
Michael, Christopher             German
  Lutheran, Congregation of Little Conawaga
  Bager            wit Fillib Eneg, Hanes Bidel


326     July 23, 1766            October 14, 1765       DD-10,76
Nicholson, John                  German
  St. Anne's
  Love            wit Jno Brown, Philip Williams


327     April 15, 1767           February 5, 1767       DD-12,607
Hivener, Adam                    German
Hivener, George                  German
Kieffer, Bartel                  German
Lingenfelter, Valentine          German
Nale, Philip                     German
  Lischy          wit Peter Erb, Johann ---


328     April 16, 1767           April 15, 1767         DD-12,608
Keys, George                     of Baltimore County, German
  Allen            wit E. Allen, Johann Ffilipe


329     May 7, 1767              September 28, 1766     DD-12,634
Appel, Catharina                 of Frederick County, German
  Lutheran, Frederick Town
  Shwordfeger    wit Joseph Sardonis, John Michl Widmeyer Jr

330    May 7, 1767              April 16, 1767            DD-12,634
Badhauer, Andrew             of Frederick County, German
 Moravian
 Krogshup      wit Lorentz Krieger, Lorentz Prozmann

331    May 7, 1767              April 16, 1767            DD-12,634
Protzman, Lewis              of Frederick County, German
 Moravian
 Krogshup      wit Lorentz Krieger, John Wolnig

332    May 7, 1767              April 16, 1767            DD-12,634
Suss, George                 of Frederick County, German
 Moravian
 Krogshup      wit Jacob Weller, Georg Herbach

333    May 7, 1767              May 3, 1767              DD-12,634
Deetz, Adam                  of Frederick County, German
Hariem, Tobias               of Frederick County, German
House, William               of Frederick County, German
Stadelmyer, David            of Frederick County, German
Wittmyer, John Michael       of Frederick County, German
 Lutheran, Frederick Town
 Shwordfeger    wit Tobias Reissner, Otto Rudolph Crecelius

334    May 7, 1767              April 19, 1767            DD-12,634
Herman, Michael              of Frederick County, German
 Reformed, Frederick County
 Longe

335    May 7, 1767              April 19, 1767            DD-12,634
Hilderbrand, Heronemas       German
Keller, John                 German
 Reformed, Frederick Town
 Longe         wit Stephen Remsperger, Jeorg Hoffman, George Lingenfelter

336    May 7, 1767              May 3, 1767              DD-12,634
Fay, Simon                   resident of Frederick Town, German
 Lutheran, Frederick Town
 Shwordfeger    wit Conrad Grosh, Tobias Reissner

337    May 7, 1767              April 5, 1767             DD-12,634
Benracth, John               German, member of our meeting
 Baptist
 G. Martin      wit --- Hueber, Johannes Horn

338    May 7, 1767              April 19, 1767            DD-12,634
Liser, Jost                  German, affirmed oath

Baptist, Frederick County
Leatherman     wit John Arnold, Lutebig Rodtrock

339    May 7, 1767              April 17, 1767            DD-12,634
Bohrer, Peter                German
Reformed, Frederick Town
Longe          wit Georg Hoffman, Jacob Huber

340    May 7, 1767              May 7, 1767              DD-12,634
Deefenback, Christian        of Germany Township, York County, German
                             also referred to as Christopher Deefenback
Lutheran, Frederick Town
Shwordfeger    wit Tobias Reissner, Otto Rudolph Crecelius

341    May 7, 1767              April 16, 1767           DD-12,634
Vertress, Hartman            of Frederick County, German
 Moravian
Krogshup       wit Lorentz Krieger, Jacob Weller

342    May 7, 1767              May 3, 1767              DD-12,634
Baulus, Nicholas             of Frederick County, German
Hinckel, George Henry        of Frederick County, German, communion only
Reesinger, John Adam         of Frederick County, German
Lutheran, Frederick Town
Shwordfeger    wit Conrad Grosh, Michael Romer

343    May 7, 1767              April 17, 1767           DD-12,634
Keller, Jacob                German
Reformed, Frederick Town
Longe          wit Stephen Rumsperger, Georg Hoffman, Georg Lingenfelter

344    May 7, 1767                                       DD-12,634
Keller, Philip

345    May 7, 1767              April 19, 1767           DD-12,634
Everhard, Jacob              German
Reformed, Frederick Town
Longe          wit Stephen Remsperger, Georg Hoffman, Henrich Shaber

346    May 7, 1767              May 3, 1767              DD-12,634
Trautman, Michael            of Frederick County, German
Lutheran, Frederick Town
Shwordfeger    wit Otto Rudolph Crecelius

347    October 1, 1767          June 21, 1767            DD-13,51/67
Badheimer, William           German, a member
Shover, Simon                German, a member

Reformed
Longe          wit Thomas Schley, Wilm Albach

348     October 1, 1767          June 7, 1767          DD-13,51/67
Kephart, Peter                    German, a member
Reformed
Longe          wit Georg Hoffman, Georg Lingenfelter

349     October 1, 1767          September 28, 1767     DD-13,51/67
Coranflow, George                 German, a member
Geeting, Henry                    German, a member
Judith, Jacob                     German, a member
Knastrig, John                    German, a member
Reformed
Longe          wit Georg Hoffman, Stephen Ramsperger

350     October 1, 1767          June 8, 1767          DD-13,51/67
Bruner, Peter                     German, a member
Reformed, Congregation on Kittocking
Longe          wit Georg Hoffman, Conrad Jung, Jacob ---

351     October 1, 1767          September 30, 1767     DD-13,51/67
Baumgertel, Ehrhard               of Frederick County, German
Beegel, David                     of Frederick County, German
Hinckel, George                   of Frederick County, German
Hinckel, Jacob                    of Frederick County, German
Stam, Adam                        of Frederick County, German
Zentbower, Martin                 of Frederick County, German
Lutheran
Shwordfeger   wit Tobias Reissner, Johan Adamsbert, Wilhelm Michel

352     October 1, 1767          August 23, 1767       DD-13,51/69
Spengle, Daniel                   German
Baptist
Rolland        wit Henrich Miller, Andreas ---, Jacob Schneider

353     October 1, 1767          August 12, 1767       DD-13,51/69
Bruder, Tobias                    German, member of the Dunkers
Reformed
Oderbein       wit --- Greind, Felde Bligel

354     April 12, 1768           April 11, 1768        DD-14,648
Miller, Nicholas                  of Baltimore County, German
St. Paul's
Chase          wit Jacob Myers, John Slater

355     May 5, 1768              April 3, 1768         DD-14,661

Benner, John            of Frederick County, German
Hoss, Jacob             of Frederick County, German
Weber, Leonnard         of Frederick County, German
  Frederick Town
  Shwordfeger

356    May 5, 1768            March 18, 1768         DD-14,661
Troxle, Abraham          of Frederick County, German, a member
  Reformed
  Boogler

357    May 5, 1768            Easter Monday last     DD-14,661
Hossler, Jacob           of Frederick County, German, a member
  Reformed, at Katockling Schoolhouse
  Longe

358    October 20, 1768                              DD-15,1
Markey, John
Souther, Christopher

359    September 7, 1768       September 7, 1768      DD-15,16
Hook, Rudolph            German
Lambert, Balser          German
Seigarsar, Felix         German
  St. Paul's
  Chase        wit Friedrich Meyer, Balser Mayer

360    September 7, 1768       September 7, 1768
Durr, Johannes Balthasar  German
Koberstein, Georg         German
Wacker, Jost              German
  Lutheran, Baltimore Town
  Kirchner      wit Conrath Conrath, Nicholas Wacker

361    September 8, 1768       September 7, 1768      DD-15,18
Vollhardt, Philip        resident of Baltimore Town, German
  Baltimore Town
  Kirchner      wit Adam Shack, Johein Crenheifer

362    September 8, 1768       September 8, 1768      DD-15,18
Bower, Daniel            German
Rinehart, Abraham        German
  St. Paul's
  Chase        wit Friedrich Meyer, Jacob Madery

363    September 14, 1768      September 13, 1768     DD-15,23
Eckhardt, Georg Adam     German

Kramer, Henrich            German
Meyer, Henrick             German
 Baltimore Town
 Kirchner        wit Arthur Coskery, --- Jones


364    October 6, 1768          July 31, 1768           DD-15,35
Smith, John                   of Frederick County, German, a member
Wohlfarht, Adam               of Frederick County, German, a member
 Lutheran, members of the Lutheran Congregation in Elizabeth Town
 Wildbahne       wit Martin Ferre, Leonhard ---


365    October 6, 1768          July 31, 1768           DD-15,35
Reydenaure, Nicholas          of Frederick County, German
 Lutheran
 Wildbahne       wit Heinrich Reitnawer


366    May 3, 1769              May 3, 1769             DD-15,333
Schmetzer, Adam               of Frederick County, German, a member
 St. John's Church, Frederick Town
 Hartwick        wit Jacob Young, Conrad Grosh


367    May 3, 1768              1st Sunday after Easter DD-15,333
Humber, Jacob                 German
 Hartwick        wit Henrich Miller, Andrew Haberly


368    (April 10, 1770)                                DD-16,3
Spittler, John                of Baltimore County


369    September 6, 1769        July 30, 1769           DD-16,12
Birkinbile, Andrew            German
 Baptist, Congregation at Conawagen
 Rohr            wit David Newman, Martin Bond


370    September 6, 1769        September 4, 1769        DD-16,12
Faubel, Jacob                 German
Franckfurter, Nicholaas       German
Kenbold, Jacob                German
Schwenck, Conrod              German
 Lutheran, Baltimore Town
 Kirchner        wit Ffilig Zittig, John Haun


371    September 7, 1769        (September 7, 1769)      DD-16,13
Hook, Jacob                   German
Hook, Joseph                  German
 (Baltimore)
 Fabery          wit Friedrich Meyer, --- Meyer

372     October 5, 1769          (October 2, 1769)        DD-16,35/36
Vickersheim, Adam               of Frederick County, German, came into this
                                County about twelve years ago
   Lutheran
Smith          wit Frantz Noll

373     April 10, 1770                                    DD-16,402
Gross, Francis
Snider, Henry
Wildemann, Jacob

374     April 14, 1770                                    DD-16,403
Williard, Elias                 of Frederick County, German
Youst, Harmond                  of Frederick County, German

375     September 13, 1770                                DD-17,2
Trajer, George                  of Baltimore County, German

376     September 14, 1770                                DD-17,3
Keysler, Jacob                  German
Leypold, John                   German
Spindler, Jacob                 German

377     April 10, 1771                                    DD-17,256
Borkly, George                  German
Heerin, Mary                    German

378     April 11, 1771                                    DD-17,256
Boyer, Malacki                  German
Morningstar, Angell             German

379     April 12, 1771                                    DD-17,257
Lamb, Conrad                    German
Moore, Stuffill                 German
Regher, Peter                   German
Rup, Jacob                      German

380     April 15, 1771                                    DD-17,258
Clantz, Jacob                   German
Fox, Mathias                    German
Guise, Peter                    German
Otto, Peter                     German

381     April 20, 1771                                    DD-17,261
Bekner, Henry                   German
Walts, Reinhard                 German

382     April 25, 1771                                        DD-17,264
Stadler, Thomas              of Charles County, German

383     September 27, 1771                                    DD-17,597
Galman, Henrich              German

384     April 15, 1772                                        DD-18,74
Beal, John                   German
Fisher, Peter                German
Fogelson, George             German
Herman, John                 German
Houptman, Henry              German
Koon, John                   German
Leydig, Jost                 German
Nicumer, Henry               German
Ulrick, Jacob                German

385     April 17, 1772                                        DD-18,74
Kirch, George

386     April 23, 1772                                        DD-18,75
Crush, Peter                 German
Fisher, Adam                 German
Haus, John                   German
Martz, Peter                 German
Reip, Valentine              German
Weis, Jacob                  German
Woolf, Michael               German

387     April 27, 1772                                        DD-18,78
Leatherman, Henry            German
Morgan, Felix                German

388     April 28, 1772                                        DD-18,79
Methet, Charles              German
Pecker, John                 German

389     April 29, 1772                                        DD-18,79
Peppla, William

390     September 8, 1772                                     DD-18,83
Grundick, John               German
Tipolet, Mary Magdaline      German

391     September 9, 1772                                     DD-18,376
Arbegast, Christopher        German
Edrion, Christian            German

Schall, Joseph                German

392    September 10, 1772                          DD-18,376
Clappert, Herman
Gref, Adam
Heiser, William
Slowder, Christian

393    September 15, 1772                          DD-18,378
Wedell, George               German
Weesner, Mathias             German

394    September 23, 1772                          DD-18,382
Bruder, Henry                of Frederick County, German

395    September 25, 1772                          DD-18,385
Frank, Peter
Frank, Philip Lawrence
Miller, Adam
Segrist, Valentine

396    April 15, 1773                             DD-19,2
Keiner, Peter                German

397    April 17, 1773                             DD-19,3
Maagg, Henrick               German
Schuffi, Johannes            German

398    April 16, 1773                             DD-19,3
Kever, Jacob                 German
Weiver, Henericus            German

399    April 21, 1773                             DD-19,5
Shover, Peter                German

400    April 22, 1773                             DD-19,5
Sibell, Henry                German
Stigar, Jordan               German

401    May 1, 1773                                DD-19,11
Weaver, George               of Frederick County, German

402    September 4, 1773                          DD-19,14
Carbeck, Valentine           of Baltimore County, German

403    September 15, 1773                         DD-19,380
Cheek, Ludwick               German

Martin, John                    German

404    September 16, 1773                          DD-19,380
Beckerum, Frederick        German
Holtz, Jacob               German
Huffman, Casper            German
Keibler, George            German
Krup, Andrew               German
Michael, Jacob             German
Schmit, Andreas            German
Schmit, Elizabeth          German
Stehly, Elizabeth          German

405    May 3, 1774                                 DD-19,585
Meddert, Henrick           German
Miller, Philip             German
Schroff, Christopherus     German
Stull, Mathias             German
Yong, George               German

406    May 4, 1774                                 DD-19,586
Baker, Henry               German
Miller, Gotlob             German
Wolf, John                 German

407    May 10, 1774                                DD-19,591
Truell, Philip             German

408    May 11, 1774                                DD-19,592
Baner, Adam                German
Beck, Andrew               German
Bringle, Christian         German
Ehhaldt, Matthew           German
Etchberger, Dewalt         German
Jung, Jacob                German
Luder, John                German
Marzahl, Philip            German
Shafter, Jacob             German
Shellery, Ulrich           German

409    May 13, 1774                                DD-19,594
Heberlin, Andrew           of Frederick County, German

410    May 20, 1774                                DD-19,597
Laterman, Frederick

411    October 14, 1774                            DD-20,3

Hyner, Nicholas · of Baltimore County, German

412 November 29, 1774 · DD-20,7
Hammond, Peter · German
Hoffman, Francis · German
Kelsor, Andrew · German
Taylor, Michael · German
Tom, Michael · German

413 March 29, 1775 · DD-20,16
Martin, Charles · German
Shaver, John · German

APPENDIX

PLACE-NAMES, CLERGYMEN, AND PARISHES

Explanatory lists of the place-names, clergymen, and Church of England parishes mentioned in the naturalization records follow. Modern spellings of place-names have been used, although some examples of the spellings which appear in the records are provided for comparison. The spellings of the clergymen's names were taken from the communion certificates. Those men for whom no sketch is given could not be traced and, evidently, were irregular, lay, or unordained ministers.

PLACE-NAMES

Antietam
A major creek in eastern Washington County flowing into the Potomac River.

Antietam Furnace
An ironworks located at the confluence of the Antietam Creek and the Potomac River in Washington County.

Catoctin
(Kittockting)
A major creek in western Frederick County; a ridge of mountains forming the eastern boundary of the valley containing the creek.

Codorus
A major creek flowing from Adams County, Pennsylvania through York County and town into the Susquehanna River; a township in York County east of Hanover touching the Maryland border.

Conewago
(Canawagda)
A creek in Adams County, Pennsylvania, west of McSherrystown, near Littlestown, flowing through York County into the Susquehanna River.

Conococheague
(Kanigochiquon)
A major creek in western Washington County flowing into the Potomac River; a dispersed settlement along the Creek; the original settlement at Williamsport.

Elizabeth Town
Hagerstown, Washington County.

Fort Frederick
French and Indian War fort in Washington County, on the Potomac River near Indian Springs.

Germany Township

A township in Adams County, Pennsylvania, containing Littlestown and touching the Maryland border.

Heidleberg Township

A township in York County, Pennsylvania, northeast of Hanover.

Hunting Creek

Two creeks (Big Hunting and Little Hunting) in western Frederick County flowing near Thurmont, Creagerstown, and Lewistown into the Monocacy River.

Mannheim Township

A township in York County, Pennsylvania, southeast of Hanover, touching the Maryland border.

Middle Creek
    (Mittee Creek)

A creek rising in southwestern Adams County, Pennsylvania, and flowing through Frederick County near Emmitsburg into Toms Creek.

Monocacy
    (Manakoese)

A river in central Frederick County flowing into the Potomac River; the first settlement in Frederick County, traditionally located near Thurmont and Creagerstown.

Mount Pleasant
  Township

A township in Adams County, Pennsylvania, east of Gettysburg.

Neapolis

Annapolis (?).

Patapsco
    (Bedepsko)

A river forming part of the boundary between Baltimore and Anne Arundel Counties and flowing into the Chesapeake Bay at Baltimore City.

Pine Run Hundred

A hundred of Frederick County, now part of Carroll County, containing Taneytown.

Pipe Creek

Big Pipe Creek - A creek in northwestern Carroll County, south of Taneytown, flowing into Double Pipe Creek.
Little Pipe Creek - A creek forming part of the boundary between Frederick and Carroll Counties, flowing into Double Pipe Creek.

Sharpsburgh

Sharpsburg, the first town laid out in Washington County.

| | |
|---|---|
| Silver Run<br>(Silber Round) | A creek in northern Carroll County flowing into Big Pipe Creek; a village near the Creek. |
| Taney Town<br>(Danys Town)<br>(Anthonis Town) | Taneytown. |
| Toms Creek | A creek rising in southwestern Adams County, Pennsylvania, flowing through Frederick County, south of Emmitsburg and into the Monocacy. |

## CLERGYMEN

| | |
|---|---|
| Allen, Bennett | Church of England; b. Hertford, England, 1737; d. England, after 1782; Rector St. Anne's Parish 1767-1768, All Saints' Parish 1768-1775. |
| Bacon, Thomas | Church of England; b. Isle of Man, England, c. 1700; d. Frederick, Md., May 24, 1768; Rector St. Peter's Parish (Talbot Co.) 1746-1758, All Saints' Parish 1759-1768. |
| Bager, George | Lutheran; b. Neiderlinzweiler, Germany, March 29, 1725; d. Hanover, Pa., June 9, 1791; Served Hanover and York, Pa., 1752-1763, 1769-1791. |
| Bauer, John Bernhard | Reformed; Active at Patapsco in 1753. |
| Beahler, Francis | Moravian; d. Lititz, Pa., 1806; Served Graceham, Frederick Co., Md., 1762-1764. |
| Beck, John Ludwig | Lutheran. |
| Bernhard, Frederick | Lutheran. |
| Boogler, Conrad<br>(Bucher) | Reformed; b. Schaffhausen, Switzerland, June 13, 1730; d. Annville, Pa., August 15, 1780; Served Frederick Co., Md., 1765-1768. |
| Bourdillion, Ben. | Church of England; d. Baltimore, January 5, 1745; Rector Somerset Parish (Somerset Co.) 1737-1739, St. John's Parish (Baltimore Co.) 1739, St. Paul's Parish 1739-1745. |

Brooke, Clement               Church of England; b. Prince George's County,
                              Md., September 1, 1730; d. November 18, 1800;
                              Probationer St. Anne's Parish 1756-1759, Curate
                              Prince George's Parish 1759-1761?.

Chandler, David               Lutheran; d. Hanover, Pa., December 1744; Served
                              Frederick County, Md., and Conewago, Pa., 1743-
                              1744.

Chase, Thomas                 Church of England; b. England 1700; d. Baltimore
                              April 4, 1779; Rector St. Paul's Parish 1745-
                              1779.

Craddock, Thomas              Church of England; b. Wolversham, England, 1718;
                              d. Baltimore, May 7, 1770; First rector of St.
                              Thomas' Parish 1745-1770.

Dowie, W(illiam)              Church of England; St. John's Parish (Queen
                              Anne's County), Durham Parish (Charles County).

Eversfield, John              Church of England; b. Turnbridge, England, 1703;
                              d. Baltimore, 1780; Served St. Paul's Parish
                              (Prince George's County) 1727-1780.

Faber, John Cristoph          Reformed; b. Mosbach, Germany, December 24, 1734;
                              d. 1796; Served Pipe Creek and Taneytown, Fred-
                              erick Co., Md., 1768-1785.

Gerock, John Siegfried        Lutheran; b. Wuertemburg, Germany; d. Baltimore,
                              1787; Served in Pennsylvania 1753-1767.

Gordon, John                  Church of England; b. Aberdeen, Scotland, 1717;
                              d. St. Michael's, Md., 1790; Rector of St, Anne's
                              Parish 1745-1749.

Gottreck, Fredsham            pseudonym of Johann Conrad Beissel.  German Bap-
                              tist; b. Eberbach, Germany, April 1690; d. Ephra-
                              ta, Pa., July 6, 1768; Founder of cloister at
                              Ephrata.

Harwich, John C.              Lutheran; b. Thueringen, Germany, January 6, 1714;
     (Hartwig)                d. Clermont, New York, July 17, 1796; Served
                              Frederick, Md., 1762, 1768-1769.

Hausihl, Berhard              Lutheran (converted to Church of England, 1785);

b. Heilbronn, Germany, 1727; d. Halifax, N. S.,
March 9, 1799; Served Frederick Co., Md., 1752-
1759.

Hornell, Nicholas        Lutheran; b. Sweden; Served York Co., Pa.,
                         1763-

Jennings, Joseph         Church of England; First rector of All Saints'
                         Parish 1742-1745.

Keene, Samuel            Church of England; b. Baltimore, May 11, 1734;
                         d. St. Michael's, Md., May 8, 1810; Rector St.
                         Anne's Parish 1762-1763.

Kirchner, John Caspar    Lutheran; d. Baltimore, 1773; Served Baltimore
                         1762-1763, York, Pa., 1763-1767.

Krogshup, Christian      Moravian; d. Bethlehem, Pa., 1785; Served
                         Graceham, Frederick Co., Md., 1764-1767.

Lake, Charles            Church of England; d. 1763; Rector of St. Anne's
                         Parish 1740-1743, St. James' Parish (Anne
                         Arundel Co.) 1749-1763.

Leatherman, Daniel       German Baptist; Served Conewago, Pa., and
                         Frederick Co., Md., 1738-1770.

Lischy, Jacob            Moravian (to c. 1747) and Reformed; b. Alsace,
                         France May 28, 1719; d. York Co., Pa., 1780;
                         Served York Co., Pa., and Frederick Co., Md.,
                         1748-1760.

Longe, Charles           Reformed; b. Innsbruch, Austria February 14,
                         1731; d. c. 1770; Served Frederick Co., Md.,
                         1766-1768.

Love, David              Church of England; Rector All Hallows Parish
                         (Anne Arundel Co.) 1765-1775.

Martin, George           German Baptist; b. Landstuhl, Germany 1715;
                         d. Ephrata, Pa., April 29, 1794; Served Cone-
                         wago, Pa., 1741-1770, Frederick Co. 1763-1770.

Martin, Nicholas         German Baptist; Served Conewago, Pa., and
                         Frederick Co., Md., c. 1770.

| | |
|---|---|
| Otterbein, P. William | Reformed; b. Dillenburg, Germany June 3, 1726; d. Baltimore November 17, 1813; Served Frederick Town and Co., 1760-1765, Baltimore 1774-1813. |
| Reiger, John Barth. | Reformed; b. Oberingelheim, Germany January 23, 1707; d. Lancaster, Pa., March 11, 1769; Served in Lancaster Co., Pa., 1745-1769. |
| Rohr, Christian | German Baptist. |
| Roland, Casper | German Baptist. |
| Schlets, Christopher | Lutheran. |
| Schmidt, Joachim Johann | |
| Shwordfeger, Samuel | Lutheran; b. Neustadt, Germany 1722; d. 1788; Served Frederick Co., Md., 1763-1768. |
| Smith, Frederick | Lutheran. |
| Steiner, Conrad | Reformed; b. Winterthur, Switzerland January 2, 1707; d. Philadelphia, July 6, 1762; Served Frederick Co., Md., 1756-1759. |
| Stoner, Jacob | Reformed. |
| Stover, John Casper Jr. | Lutheran; b. Luedorff, Germany December 21, 1707. |
| Templeman, Edward | |
| Waldschmidt, John | Reformed; b. Dillenburg, Germany August 6, 1724; d. Cocalico, Lancaster Co., Pa., September 14, 1786; Served Lancaster Co., Pa. |
| Wildbahne, Charles | Lutheran; d. 1804; Served Frederick Co., Md., 1768-1782. |
| Williamson, Alex | Church of England; b. Calvert Co., Md., c. 1727; d. Georgetown, D. C. 1787; Rector St. Anne's Parish 1759-1761, Rock Creek Parish (D.C.) 1761-1776. |
| Wirt, John Conrod (Wuertz) | Reformed; b. Zurich, Switzerland November 30, 1706; d. York, Pa., September 21, 1763; Served York, Pa., 1762-1763. |

Zahn, John Michael      Moravian; b. Sungheim, Germany; d. Bethlehem, Pa., 1787; Served Graceham, Frederick Co., Md., 1758-1762.

## PARISHES

St. Anne's Parish      Anne Arundel County; established 1692; parish church located in Annapolis.

St. Paul's Parish      Baltimore City and County; established 1692; parish church located in Baltimore City.

All Saints' Parish      Frederick County; established 1742; parish church located in Frederick Town.

St. Thomas' Parish      Baltimore County; established 1745; parish church located in Garrison, northwest of Baltimore City.

## REFERENCES

Richards, George W., ed., Ministers of The German Reformed Congregations in Pennsylvania and Other Colonies in the Eighteenth Century by William J. Hinke, Lancaster, Pa., 1951.

Rightmyer, Nelson Waite, Maryland's Established Church, Baltimore, 1956.

Weis, Frederick Lewis, The Colonial Clergy of Maryland, Delaware, and Georgia, Lancaster, Mass., 1950.

The Maryland Historical Records Survey Project, Inventory of the Church Archives of Maryland, Protestant Episcopal Diocese of Maryland, Baltimore, 1940.

# INDEX TO ALIENS IN DENIZATIONS AND NATURALIZATIONS

| | | | |
|---|---|---|---|
| Hesselius, Gustavus | N47 | Hossler, Jacob | 357 |
| Hesselius, Mary | N47 | Houbman, Jacob | 139 |
| Heuster, Francis | 147 | Houptman, Henry | 384 |
| Heyell, John George | 7 | House, John | 5 |
| Hinckel, George | 351 | House, William | 333 |
| Hinckel, George Henry | 342 | Hout, George | 108 |
| Hinckel, Jacob | 351 | Hover, Vandal | 292 |
| Hickerel, Herman | 296 | Hower, Michael | 325 |
| Hicleman, Michael | 243 | Hoyl, Andrew | 321 |
| Hildebrand, see Yeildinbrand | 242 | Huber, Adam | 253 |
| Hildebrand, John | 191 | Huber, Adam | 299 |
| Hilderbrand, Heronemas | 335 | Huber, Peter | 299 |
| Hill, Peter | 322 | Huber, Ulrich | 295 |
| Hirsh, Conrad | 208 | Huber, Ulrich | 319 |
| Hivener, Adam | 327 | Huebner, Adam | 246 |
| Hivener, George | 327 | Huebner, Michael | 246 |
| Hobre, Andrew | 15 | Huffener, Melechior | 268 |
| Hochel, Justice | 170 | Huffman, Casper | 404 |
| Hoffman, Adam | 296 | Huffman, George | 86 |
| Hoffman, Francis | 412 | Humber, George | 367 |
| Hoffman, Georg | 259 | Humbert, William | 191 |
| Hoffman, Henry | 296 | Humer, Jacob | 204 |
| Hoffman, John | 18 | Hummel, John | 302 |
| Hoffman, Peter | 296 | Huntz, Devalt | 141 |
| Hofman, Leonard | 123 | Hupp, Augustus | 298 |
| Holland, John Francis | N35 | Hush, Valentine | 229 |
| Holts, Jacob | 292 | Huzel, John George | 7 |
| Holtz, Benedict | 100 | Hyle, John | 213 |
| Holtz, Jacob | 404 | Hyner, Nicholas | 411 |
| Holzman, Frederick | 195 | Hysing, Jacob | 282 |
| Hone, Gasper | 292 | Hysler, Nicholas | 292 |
| Honerkin, Jacob | 117 | Hysson, Paulser | 147 |
| Honey, George | 23 | | |
| Hoofman, John | 23 | Ibach, Jacob | 64 |
| Hoofman, Peter | 14 | Imbert, Andrew | N22 |
| Hooghe, William | 295 | Irish, Francis | 80 |
| Hook, Jacob | 371 | Isagar, Jonathan | 15 |
| Hook, Joseph | 371 | Israollo, Angel | 19 |
| Hook, Rudolph | 359 | | |
| Hool, Andreas | 155 | Jacob, Franciscus | 268 |
| Hoolf, Jacob | 26 | Jacob, Martin | 313 |
| Hoopman, Jacob | 159 | Jacobson, Jeffrey | N 8 |
| Hoover, Leonhard | 178 | Jacobson, Peter | D 3 |
| Hopper, Cornelius | 292 | Jarboe, John | D 4 |
| Horch, Elias | 31 | Jarboe, John | N 2 |
| Horch, Johannes Elias | 46 | Jeem, John | 167 |
| Hoss, Jacob | 355 | Jesseroon, Michael | 107 |

| | | | |
|---|---|---|---|
| Nomers, John | N 8 | Pickenpagh, Leonard | 197 |
| Nunemaker, Jacob | 248 | Pickler, Mark | 9 |
| | | Pinckly, John | 68 |
| Occulberry, Abraham | 296 | Piper, William | 230 |
| Odenbaugh, Jonas | 231 | Polsell, Peter | 112 |
| Oeth, John | N48 | Pope, John Grisman | 171 |
| Oleg, Sebastian | N30 | Pott, Conrod | 76 |
| Onstend, George | 213 | Potts, Ludwick | 261 |
| Opercock, Jacob | 213 | Poulson, Andrew | N16 |
| Ostertoghr, Christian | 98 | Poussum, Lawrance | 221 |
| Othason, Otho | N32 | Pouston, John | D11 |
| Ott, Michael | 298 | Powell, Barnard | 296 |
| Otto, Matthias | 263 | Powell, Philip | 296 |
| Otto, Peter | 380 | Power, Henry | 170 |
| Ouldson, John | N20 | Powlis, Jacob | 216 |
| Ouldson, Peter | N13 | Priggs, John | 28 |
| Overard, Peter | N42 | Protzman, Lawrence | 51 |
| | | Protzman, Lewis | 331 |
| Packett, David | N42 | Puchie, Mathias | 149 |
| Pacquett, Daniell | N37 | Putman, Andrew | 193 |
| Pagett, David | N39 | | |
| Pagett, Eliza | N39 | Rack, Georg Jacob | 63 |
| Pagett, Maudlin | N39 | Rashoon, Stephen | N40 |
| Panz, Adam | 271 | Rau, Andreas | 135 |
| Parandier, John | N45 | Rauh, Jacob | 83 |
| Parandier, James | N45 | Raybuck, John | 188 |
| Parks, John  see Jarboe | N 2 | Rayman, William | N56 |
| Peane, Anne | N12 | Raymel, Philip | 306 |
| Peane, James | N12 | Reber, Christoffel | 263 |
| Peane, Magdelen | N12 | Reeber, William | 306 |
| Pecker, John | 388 | Reehl, Frederick | 304 |
| Pecker, Peter | 296 | Rees, Adam | 84 |
| Pence, Michael | 145 | Reesinger, John Adam | 342 |
| Pentz, Adam | 203 | Regher, Peter | 379 |
| Peppla, William | 389 | Reichhardt, Jacob | 63 |
| Peters, Christian | N57 | Reichart, Jacob | 62 |
| Peterson, Cornelius | N 8 | Reinhard, Georg | 54 |
| Peterson, Hans | N 8 | Reip, Valentine | 386 |
| Peterson, Mathias | N 5 | Reis, Henry | 81 |
| Peterson, Mathias | N16 | Reislin, Matthew | 2 |
| Peterson, Peter | N 5 | Remespergher, George | 102 |
| Pfeiffer, Henrick | 39 | Remschberger, Stephan | 101 |
| Pfiffer, Jacob | 284 | Renner, Adam | 295 |
| Pfister, Henrick | 167 | Rensperger, Stephen | 263 |
| Pflubach, Jacob | 47 | Reydenaure, Nicholas | 365 |
| Philips, Nicholas | 125 | Reyley, Burghart | 239 |
| Philpock, John | 144 | Reyley, John | 239 |

# INDEX TO WITNESSES TO COMMUNIONS